MIND GAMES

MIND GAMES

THE UPS AND DOWNS
OF LIFE AND FOOTBALL

NEVILLE SOUTHALL

HarperCollins*Publishers*

HarperCollins*Publishers*
1 London Bridge Street
London SE1 9GF

www.harpercollins.co.uk

First published by HarperCollins*Publishers* 2020

1 3 5 7 9 10 8 6 4 2

© Neville Southall 2020
Poems © Anne-Marie Silbiger 2020

Neville Southall asserts the moral right to be
identified as the author of this work

A catalogue record of this book is
available from the British Library

ISBN 978-0-00-840373-7

Printed and bound in Great Britain by
CPI Group (UK) Ltd, Croydon

MIX
Paper from
responsible sources
FSC™ C007454

This book is dedicated to anyone who
suffers, whatever their age, gender, sexuality,
race or situation. Please know that you
are not alone.

CONTENTS

INTRODUCTION
LIFE AND FOOTBALL

There are four elements of my personality that I hold most dear. The first three are trust, loyalty and honesty, and I don't think you can have the first two without the third. If someone has something brutal to say but I trust them implicitly and believe that they're loyal to me, I'd much rather that they say it to me straight than keep it hidden.

The fourth element is that I've always believed it important to have an open mind, to realise that you don't know everything. Because I've discovered, and am still discovering, that I know absolutely fuck-all. And so everything I do now involves learning as much as I can about people and about their lives.

I find discovering – and being allowed by them to discover – things about people to be incredibly interesting, and it disheartens me that not everyone feels the same way. People should be open-minded. If they don't know about something, then they should make it their job to find out rather than either closing themselves off to it or, worse, spouting a view about something that they're not educated on. I've been burnt a few times where I've had opinions on subjects that I didn't know enough about, so the only answer was to educate myself. Ironically, education then reminds us how much we don't know.

I had the values of my parents hardwired into me. I think that's how good parenting works, and goodness knows I'm not perfect. My mum and dad were great parents to me, because they lived by good values. Having said that, my dad came home from the war, where he'd been shot at, and he never spoke about it. He had been taught that the best way to process his feelings, his fears and his experiences was to bury them. That is what society preached.

I believe that the lack of communication hampered his generation badly, although people might not have appreciated this at the time. I don't remember anyone ever asking my dad a single question about what he'd been through. I certainly didn't. Nobody ever sat him down and asked if he was OK. We just assumed that if he wanted to talk about it, then he'd come to us. But he signed up to the army as soon as he could, with the idea that war would be a bit of fun and a chance to enjoy comradeship with others like him. And it became something far more serious than they had ever been led to believe or were prepared for.

The mentality of soldiers at war has always interested me. I read a book the other month about people who killed in war, what their feelings were afterwards and how they managed – or didn't manage – to process them. There was a Japanese guy who was talking about being indoctrinated to hate the Chinese. His first bayonet practice was stabbing Chinese people. It became nothing. The army went into villages, raped the women, killed everybody. One day they were walking along a cliff and saw a woman carrying a baby. They were ordered to capture them. The woman wouldn't stop crying, so one of the soldiers threw the baby over the cliff and the woman jumped after it. Having seen all of that horror, and been an active part of it, how could you ever cope?

When my dad was sat there waiting to fight, what was that like for him? How could he cope with being so helpless, when the only question of the day was whether he would live or die? When he had no choice but to carry on and continue to be strong – or be ostracised as a traitor? What goes through your mind when you're eating your breakfast each morning? How do you walk in a line towards such unspeakable danger? These are human beings.

My dad was lucky – he got out. But the mentality of these people is extraordinary. They rarely processed it until it was too late, and they were expected to come home and fit in with normal daily life. The provisions were not there for them to do anything else, and we owe it to them not to make the same mistake with the current generation of young people who experience unspeakable things.

I like to think of myself as an experiment. How do you find out what works for you, and what makes you happier and a better person? I've learnt that the best way is to work on new strategies to solve problems and find out which are successful. It's all a process of trying, failing and succeeding, of living and learning. That applied to my football career, and what I do now. They might be very different careers – and in some ways I've lived two lives – but the principles are the same.

With mental health issues, I have to think the same way. Approach it as a scientist would: if we start trying something and it doesn't work, we'll move on to something else and continue the cycle. If one of the things we try works, then great – we know that works. But let's try something else too and see if we can make things even better, knowing we have an alternative solution if not.

As a footballer, you're basically taught not to think about much at all off the pitch, and that cannot be healthy. What did I have to think about? I went into training, I did something that I really enjoyed but which came naturally to me. Someone told me what I was doing the next day and someone told me what I was doing on Saturday. The only time when I had to think was on the drive home. And when I got home, I didn't want to do much thinking because I wanted to be rested and ready for the next match. Football challenges you in areas such as confidence, fear, pressure and motivation, but it all becomes part of one mass, one process.

You live your life around games. If you have a day off, fine. If you don't have a day off, fine. But it doesn't really change anything. You go to the airport, and someone from the club has your passport because they believe that you're too stupid to keep it yourself and hand it to the customs officer without losing it. They tell you where to sit and how long to sit for.

I didn't like lots of structure in my life, and I still don't. A lot of footballers don't, which might sound surprising. If a manager came into the dressing room and started giving me too many instructions just before kick-off, I thought, 'Look, I'm going to stop goals going in. You really don't need to give me lots of shit to do, because I'll always just do the best I can.' By the end I didn't even really like team meetings.

I was always interested in the mentality of the manager in the ten minutes they have with the team directly before kick-off. They have to give the same message, but how do they do it in different ways to keep it fresh? That's why Alex Ferguson was so brilliant, because he used different voices and different gears and different coaches. He kept changing to guarantee an impact. So if he took his squad to the same place three or four times, the message would be the same but delivered in a slightly different way. It all comes down to communication.

You get to the ground and there are people there that matter to you, but the thing that matters most is the match. I never thought about the fans, the public or anything – I just did whatever I needed to do to be the best that I could be. If I thought it was best that I went to the match early, I went early. If I thought it best that I went a little later, I went a little later. That's a very selfish attitude, but you're taught to be selfish. You have total tunnel vision. And the indirect result of that is that when anyone tells you to do something out of the ordinary, some cannot cope – and they kick up a fuss.

I know what I don't know; that has always been one of my greatest strengths. I don't have all the answers, or even half of them. I know what I know, and know how to use that to help myself and others, but I also know where my gaps are, in knowledge and in expertise. If you know what you don't know, it's far easier to be an open person than if you think you know everything. It's easier said than done, and it takes work, but it's worth it.

That's why Twitter has been brilliant for me. Because if I don't know something, and feel like I owe it to others to gain a greater understanding of it, I can quickly find someone who knows more and ask them. And at the start of each chapter of this book is a short tip or piece of advice from some of the people who I have relied upon in my education. When I reached out, they responded. Each of them does exceptional work in campaigning or raising awareness. At the end of each chapter is a short poem by the brilliant Anne-Marie Silbiger, who gave up her time for free to compose each one from scratch for the book. These are just some of the people I have met through Twitter.

I think the principle of reaching out to educate yourself applies to football too. There are too many people doing jobs in which they have to pretend to be experts on subjects that they don't know enough about, and that leads to people leading others without having the best tools to help them succeed. At times in this book I'll talk about football and at times I'll talk about 'normal' life, but there's a crossover at every point. What applies to football and to footballers invariably applies to life.

The main reason that I wanted to write this book is because people don't just want to listen to someone talking shite. They want solutions, or potential solutions. They know what the problem is, and they're desperate for someone to help them deal with it. But I also wanted to get across that I'm not just an ex-footballer. In fact I'm not a footballer at all anymore. I work in a special school, a school where it takes so much time and effort to get anything for the kids. I'm also a human being, and the public too quickly forgets that about our sportspeople and celebrities. We suffer the same high and lows, and are forced to deal with both in a very public arena.

People want some strategies. I believe – or hope – that I have some ideas on a number of subjects and that I can offer solutions. I'm not perfect, and I don't have all the answers, but I want to start a conversation about how we approach certain topics and certain communities within society. We have let the most vulnerable communities in our society down for too long, and in truth this means that it isn't a society at all.

In writing this book, I wanted to give myself a place where I can hopefully prove that a former footballer like me doesn't just have to be defined by the job they had in the past, but also by the way in which they approached life after it. If this book can be helpful in offering an insight into that, brilliant. And if I can use the platform that football gave me to get through to people on a number of issues that I consider to be important – more important than football – then I'm very lucky.

I also wanted to create something that told people who are struggling that there are others who are thinking of them, so they know that they're not alone; after all, it's far too easy to ignore people and live in our own bubble. In putting pen to paper in this way, I hope to raise awareness and tell those who don't think of others enough that they should. Because that's the only way that our country will become more tolerant. Only by being kinder on an individual basis can we help to create a society that relies upon community and consideration for others.

This extraordinary year in our lives, during which we were forced to live in lockdown conditions and in fear of a deadly virus, has only increased that need to look after our own well-being and to increase our empathy and sympathy for those around us. I honestly believe that out of such misery something beautiful can be built, a society in which those who are struggling are not deliberately ignored or stigmatised. But it will take fight and unity, both on a personal and a community level.

So this is me. This book is as close to me as you can get. I played football for twenty-odd years, but that isn't me now. I've done that. I've been asked 3,000 times what my favourite game was and I've answered that question 3,000 times. Football has certainly helped me in the second part of my life, and for that I will always be grateful. But there are other things that I'm interested in. I want to help people, and I want everyone else to help other people too.

1
CONFIDENCE

'We fear failure and criticism, but have faith in
yourself and show yourself compassion and
still do what you want to do.'
Saiqa Naz, cognitive behavioural therapist
(#AskSaiqa)

Every footballer goes through periods when they're low on confidence, but I don't think we view them in such psychological terms at the time. For me, I was just either going through good periods on the pitch or bad periods, and I tried to keep an eye on my outlook accordingly. Fortunately, I had more good times than bad.

If I was doing well, I tried not to think about my mood at all because I never needed to – football ruled all. But even if I was going through a patch of poor form, I never sat down and thought, 'Right, I'm low on confidence now and that needs to change,' because it was only ever correlated with my performances. Make sure they were good, or improve them if I needed to, and the confidence would look after itself. That was one benefit of being so obsessed with my career: football led everything else.

When you're doing well on the pitch, nothing else matters.

The best way I can describe it is that it feels like you're flying slightly above the ground, with the usual roadblocks of life unable to affect you. The highs that success gave me meant that I was happy every day, as they made everything else fall into place. During those times, even losing a match didn't matter. I just saw it as a blip in a continuous upward trend.

When you're a young player or young person, you're desperate to make an impression, so you're happy to be relied upon and take responsibility. You want to impress your friends, impress the people at work, impress your manager. As a goalkeeper, that's particularly true because you know that pulling off great saves is the best way to get praise. Because most journalists and pundits have never been goalkeepers, they're impressed by the spectacular. So when I was starting out at Everton in 1981, I was desperate to be busy.

As you get older and wiser, you realise that it's better to be quiet as a goalkeeper. From then on, I honestly wouldn't mind if I never even had a single save to make. I didn't want to do anything – no dives, no catches, no chivvying of my team-mates. If the defence could stop me having to get involved in the game, I was happy. It meant the team were performing perfectly. Of course, people would then say that I'd had an easy match, but it merely proved that our preparation had been perfect: I'd organised the defence well and they'd protected me.

That can be a tricky thing to appreciate, psychologically, because people are hardwired to be busy. It's not in our nature to do nothing, and being busy builds confidence. As a goalkeeper, you're like an emergency doctor on call, ready to help if something happens – and being paid for doing so – but actually better off not being needed at all.

When I first broke into the Everton team in 1981, I didn't do that well. I don't think it was related to confidence; I was just making the wrong decisions. I think if you're truly low on confidence then it ends up with you not making any decisions at all, rather than making the wrong decisions. I was making decisions, but too often choosing badly. Working out which are the right decisions to make and which aren't becomes a semi-automatic learning process, because experience shapes your behaviour and decision-making. Practice does make perfect, and always has.

What drove me on in that difficult initial period was my determination that I didn't want my career to be defined negatively. I knew that if my poor decision-making on the pitch carried on for too much longer that I'd lose my best chance to establish myself in the First Division (as the Premier League was known at the time). So I needed to change it. I always wanted to be the best, so I redoubled my efforts. Now you might still think, 'Oh fuck, not another mistake' when they happen, but the determination to reach the end goal carries you through.

Being confident doesn't mean that you won't make mistakes, because everyone does in every job. I'm a firm believer that only by going through a shit time can you be prepared for the next time it comes around. It helps to give you a sense of perspective. Confidence is having the faith in yourself that you'll learn from your mistakes, not that you won't make any.

Some players find that harder than others, of course. Some beat themselves up for mistakes and in doing so make things harder for themselves the next time they find themselves in a similar situation. I also think that a lack of confidence can often lead to people looking for others to help them out, including their teammates on the pitch. How often do we see a player going quiet in a match when it's not going their way? But the confident people will demand the ball, continue to take shots, try to create chances or come and claim crosses. Their confidence shouts louder than their mistakes.

Working through things yourself, however hard, is one of the keys to establishing confidence. If you prove to yourself that you can solve a problem, move on from it and put it behind you, it stands to reason that the next time you suffer a setback it will scare you less because you already have proof that you can respond to it positively.

When I was going through a tough time on the pitch and I wanted to try something that I thought might help me improve, I'd go straight to the manager or the goalkeeping coach, make the suggestion and explain why I thought it might work. Almost every time, they'd allow me to do it. And why wouldn't they? Nobody knew my game better than me.

Maybe it's easier for a goalkeeper, because the chances are that the manager isn't a goalkeeping expert. But some gaffers can have set ideas about what a goalkeeper should be, based on who they have managed during their career, and that can put barriers up. Luckily there was almost always a circle of trust at Everton, where the coaches had faith in me getting it right and I trusted them enough that I would take their advice on board.

But my independence did occasionally get me into trouble. On the opening day of the 1990/91 season we were playing Leeds United at Goodison, and the team produced an awful performance. We were 2–0 down at half-time, and after going into the dressing room I realised that I needed to clear my head, away from the rest of the lads. I went and sat against one of the goalposts and just tried to get my head together to perform in the second half.

I'd actually done exactly the same thing a year earlier, during an away game at Wimbledon, but this time it became a story. I suppose the fact that it was at Goodison made it notorious, but the press picked up on it and turned it into a massive issue. They said that I had gone back out on the pitch in protest at Colin Harvey's management. That was total bollocks, because it was just about clearing my head and restoring my confidence, but I can now see that it was badly timed.

Colin rang me that evening after the match, and he was furious about my actions. I explained the situation and my reasoning, which seemed to appease him, but when I saw him the next day he told me that the club was fining me two weeks' wages and suspending me from all club activity.

Given that I thought I'd been mistreated, having explained myself fully, I asked my agent to ask Colin if I could go on holiday if he didn't want me around the club. I had no intention of doing anything of the sort – I hated holidays and wanted to train more than anything else in the world – but it did the trick. Colin was soon on the phone to tell me to come into training on the Monday, and I started the next game against Coventry City. I never did it again.

If confidence was a relatively simple thing for me to manage, it clearly isn't the same for everyone. When I was coaching the goalkeepers at Bradford City in 2000, we did a survey of the players and asked them to describe how they felt at various times during the course of the matchday: on the way to the game, in the dressing room just before they went on and when they kicked off. Their answers were very different. Some players built themselves up over time, feeling nervous in the morning but pumped and ready by kick-off. Others woke up feeling great, but that ebbed away as kick-off approached. Some needed an early positive piece of action in the game before they felt ready. Others didn't.

All this probably seems obvious if you actually think about it, but it proved that every player was different. They did whatever they had to do to try to feel as comfortable as possible so that they performed at their best, and no one single approach would have worked for all of them. As coaches we had to understand this, allowing the players a degree of independence to enable them all to be as relaxed and confident as possible. If one goalkeeper needed an early touch of the ball, the defenders might give him a few backpasses to get him into the game. If another suffered from their confidence ebbing away just before the game, one of the coaches might have a one-to-one with them at 2.30pm and offer them encouragement.

Superstitions are often derided or mocked because they seem silly to those who don't require them. Putting your shin pads on a certain way or the team coming out onto the pitch in a certain order can't affect the result of the match, these people will say, so you're just relying on meaningless nonsense. But things like this are about the potential impact they have; they're done to keep a player within a comfort zone and the right frame of mind to attack the challenge to come.

Psychologically, that helps to build confidence and so they become valuable. As long as the superstitions don't dominate your match preparation, why wouldn't you do it?

Personally, I didn't really have any superstitions because for me it was all about physical and mental preparation, but I'd never criticise a player that did. You do whatever it is you need to do to feel good when the match begins. Of course, you can't solely rely on a superstition as some magical good-luck charm that will sort everything out; but if it helps give you an extra few per cent, then go for it.

There's also no magic formula for building up confidence. It's about people, and understanding how they tick. That example of managing confidence on a matchday at Bradford City is just one way in which it makes a difference. If you can put your jigsaw together as a team, understand the nuances of the personalities of the players in that team and allow them to express themselves, you've got a good chance. If you're trying to force players into a system and just expecting them to gel with each other organically, with no micromanagement, you're onto a loser.

But although this indicates that coaches play a vital role in building – and maintaining – confidence, the best players are the ones who look for solutions on the pitch to problems that present themselves. They obviously also need the talent to execute the solution, but thinking quickly is half the battle. Let's say I'm a full-back who has been told to switch the play to the opposite flank when I get to the halfway line or pass it into central midfield. That's fine, but if I also have the aware-ness to spot that the midfield is cramped and that there's a space down the right, I'll exploit that and surge down the wing even if this is not normally my role. The key lies in creating players who have the freedom of expression to solve those micro situations, and that comes from living and learning.

I remember the golfer Lee Trevino; he'd do shots that nobody else could do. It was all about vision, freedom of expression and confidence. He just saw things in a way that others couldn't and so he practised them, and was therefore able to be confident even when attempting the unusual or risky. Lionel Messi is the best player in the world not just because of his talent but because of his brain. He's able to see a problem or an opportunity and solve or exploit it better – and more quickly – than anyone else.

Every player at the top level has talent, but it isn't just about natural talent. It's about managing the person to get the most out of that talent, to get them feeling confident and allowing them freedom of expression, then fitting together players with slightly different levels of talent that work best together to create the best team.

I really think that it's getting harder and harder for coaches to do that successfully, because it requires management of the personalities of the players in the team. Managers have far less power over the players than they used to. If a player gets fined a week's wages for failing to listen to instructions, does it really make as much of a difference when the salaries are so high and their agent will be able to kick up a fuss and cause problems for the club anyway?

So the only way you can do it in the modern age is by creating a philosophy – a team spirit and style of play – that is so attractive to players that you persuade everyone to buy into it, thus creating something close to a universal confidence among the squad. That's exactly what Howard Kendall did at Everton and what Liverpool have done under Jürgen Klopp. Everyone leaves their ego at the door and is given the freedom to express themselves. They all know that they have the manager's trust, and this automatically makes them feel confident.

It's also vital to remember that confidence isn't just affected by what happens on the pitch, even though that was almost always the case for me. Don't fall into the trap as a manager of preparing for matchday and forgetting about the players' lives outside the game. If someone's kid is ill, or they're having problems at home, it will obviously affect them on the pitch. It's the same in every line of work.

Let's say a player has a new baby that has been quite poorly. The player isn't getting much sleep as a result and is putting far more work in at home than they normally would. This means that they're more tired, and so training reduces their energy levels more than it usually would. Come matchday, they have less residual energy and so they make mistakes that they normally wouldn't make. That's going to kill the confidence of a player. It also puts a greater strain on their home life, because the player has evidence that it has affected his work.

When I was playing, this sort of situation could be very hard for players. You were hardwired to simply plough on through any domestic issues and keep them to yourself. But if off-pitch issues *were* affecting your performances, you'd quickly be dropped. At the time, an appearance bonus of £200 might make a huge difference to your lifestyle, which would only exacerbate the confidence issue. Perhaps a potential suitor might be put off signing you because of a period of inconsistent form. It's easy to see how whole careers can be shaped by the minutiae of daily life.

But in some ways, I think players in my day at the top level were a little more resilient. In the 1980s, there was much more variety on matchday. We had to adapt to different pitches, different balls and completely different conditions. Some grounds might be open at the corners, so the wind would whip through. There were plastic pitches, which changed how the ball bounced and how you dived. We might play on what were basically mud baths during the winter. Clubs would choose their own match balls, which moved differently through the air. The atmosphere at some grounds was really intense, at others less so.

All this has largely been lost. Plenty of stadiums look identical to one another, and every match ball is standardised. The pitches are all kept in incredible condition, because that's what managers and players like; you never get a mud bath these days. And the atmospheres around the country are virtually the same. There's very few places that would really intimidate a player now.

You hear managers moaning now if they play away in Europe or in the domestic cup competitions and the pitch is bobbly or sandy or muddy, because they've grown accustomed to everything being just so. But that variety was useful for players. It taught us to be adaptable, to cope in unexpected and imperfect scenarios.

It also made us resilient. The pitches we played on throughout the winter would sap our energy. The boots we wore would be heavy, caked in mud. But our bodies learnt to cope – they had to. In 1984/85 I played seventy matches for Everton and Wales in ten different countries. In the absence of the physiotherapists, nutritionists and expert medics that clubs use today, that was a long season.

Players now are gym-fit, but I'm not sure that their bodies are as resilient. Of course the pace of the football is more intense, but I think it was more physical when I played and the facilities that players were able to lean on were scarcer. I hear about many more players now complaining of tiredness, but when I played fatigue just wasn't a thing. Nobody ever asked if you were tired. You just played and played, for better or worse.

One truly positive change in football between then and now is the increased use of sports psychologists and the difference they can make to a player's confidence. The idea of psychological help didn't really exist when I was playing, and many people would have scoffed at it. Instead we were subject to a pretty simple process: play well and you could stay in the team and at the club; play badly and you'd be binned. The rest was just noise to be ignored.

In fact, you weren't ever really expected to talk about anything at all. If you were injured, you didn't show that you were hurt and just got on with it. If you were going through something, you concentrated on the football and vowed not to let it show. That's just how it was.

When I started doing the work I do now, it became clear to me very quickly that there were players who could have benefited hugely from getting help. That wasn't necessarily the senior players, because I probably still don't know what some of them were going through, but we had quite a few apprentices who didn't make the grade but might have with a little more guidance and support.

I remember one trainee who was put on a diet because he needed to lose a few pounds. He'd come in every morning and have his breakfast at the training ground, and then have his lunch after training and go home. The club spoke to his family, and it turned out that they were making him sandwiches for the train journey to training in the morning, and after a big tea he'd eat two Mars bars. So he did need to shift some weight.

Two weeks later, the guy was basically only eating two apples a day to try to lose it, and he couldn't last on the pitch. He had no energy whatsoever. He eventually left the club because he never rediscovered his form. Nobody ever sat down with him and asked why he was eating badly, or if he comfort ate to cope with things or had ever addressed the fact that his solution was so extreme. With a little help, he might have been able to find a balanced solution that also addressed the root cause. But he just lurched from one extreme to the other.

We had another apprentice, and when he came in he looked really good. But on a pre-season training run he got beaten by Jimmy Gabriel, who was the assistant manager and must have been in his mid-fifties by then. We asked how he'd managed to lose to Jimmy and his answer was that he could easily have beaten him but that he just wasn't that bothered, so he let Jimmy win.

He was a goalkeeper, and one day in training he said that he'd been playing against Manchester United's youth team on the Saturday and had saved a shot. Saving the shot made him laugh so much that he forgot to get up and save the rebound, and the United striker scored.

I remember telling him that he had to go away over the summer and maintain his fitness and work on improving by himself, and I gave him loads of drills to practise. He came back for pre-season training and he could barely do a press-up. He was so weak physically that it was obvious that he hadn't done a minute of exercise over the entire break.

Now those two were good kids, and good players too. They could have made it, but they were never going to because both needed support from within the club and within the game to give them that edge. One needed support to talk through his eating and extreme diet, and the other needed to discuss why he didn't have the will to improve or better himself. Perhaps a sports psychologist wouldn't have solved the issue, but the pair of them didn't even get that chance. There was nobody for either of them to turn to; they had to work it all out themselves.

Every player goes through things, because they're human beings and that's the reality of being human. It's sometimes extremely hard to work through problems without any outside help, and if you do have to work through them on your own, it takes time. But in that apprentice environment, you got very little time because there was always someone ready to take your place and you were being judged all the while. Without the support network, those who had problems were starting from behind the line – and they ended up getting lost.

Some stuff you can work out yourself, but sometimes you just need someone to talk to. I don't even think that every time it requires a trained psychologist; a pair of ears will do just fine. Someone to listen, who won't judge you, who won't say too much to you and won't share what you've told them in confidence, but just hears what you've got to say. Sometimes when you talk through something or write it down, you identify the issues and can solve the problem. But nobody did that with those apprentices – or with us as players. I'm lucky that I was able to process things pretty well myself, but it would still have been good to have someone that did that. Someone independent who just listened to you.

It all comes down to fate. Those apprentices could have met people along the way, outside the club, who gave them that time and space to work through things, who could have helped them and set them on a different path. In some respects, the lack of such people defined their lives.

I think that's where I can help people. I don't claim to be a qualified counsellor, but I am prepared to listen to people and give them time. I'm prepared to hear what they have to say, and I try to come up with potential solutions. Maybe the lack of that support when I played football has made me better at that.

The most important aspect of confidence is its infectious nature. You can tell immediately when a club is in great form and the mood is high by looking at the training-ground car park in the morning. It will be packed half an hour before players are due in, because everyone wants to impress and become an integral part of something successful. When things are going badly, however, while some players will still stay

longer at the end of training, others will want to leave immediately. Although they know they have to be there, they might
want to escape if there's a negative atmosphere around the
club.

The notion of self-fulfilling confidence can be really useful.
If you have the total respect of a squad that has bought into
your philosophy, you might want to allow them to have a few
days off – tell them to go away and do some light fitness work
by themselves, but mainly just have a few days in the sun and
relax. They won't do anything foolish to undermine morale
and will come back refreshed, having spent some time with
their families and feeling buoyed by the fact that the manager
clearly trusts them.

I don't think we see enough of that micromanagement in
other industries. It's perhaps because people just don't have
the time or the budgets to commit the resources to it, but its
absence creates a workplace culture in which people can
become incredibly dispirited. You have people who work
their arses off in their jobs, and occasionally it would be clever
if the people above them could recognise that and make a
gesture.

Little things make a huge difference. One day, if a manager
approached someone and said, 'Look, you've had a banging
headache all day, just go home half an hour early,' how much
would that motivate someone? You'd get far more than your
thirty minutes back from them because they'd feel energised
by it. It sends them the message that they aren't just a drone
working without recognition.

Say somebody has had a crap time at home for one reason
or another. Find out what their favourite flowers are, or what

kind of chocolate bar or sandwich they like, and bring them something in. You can do so much for that person's well-being with a single gesture. They'll feel valued and cared for, and will repay you in the same way.

People often don't do this kind of thing, because they feel – not unreasonably – that they're too busy to think about it. But every kid that comes into our school is given an individual learning package, and with that we can tailor their education to their needs. Yet we don't seem to ever do that in later life. It all just gets lost in the noise.

It's odd, because not doing it is also so counter-productive. If you feel that people above you care about you, you'll be predisposed to give them more and be confident about yourself. You're sure that others have your back. You'll also become more likely to express yourself because you believe that they know you well enough to realise that any mistake wasn't intentional, and you'll feel better about being able to rectify it anyway. It's so much easier to be confident in yourself if you have faith that others are confident in you.

I'm a firm believer that you have to learn to take the rough with the smooth. That doesn't just apply to football or other sports but to all areas of life. People who can appreciate the good times but not get carried away by success are more likely to be happy. And people who can cling on to the memories and the lessons of those good times and use them to help them through a rough patch are far more likely to be able to come through the other side better for the experience.

You just have to treat both extremes as similarly as possible and stay on an even keel. Allow yourself to get carried away when things are going well and you risk taking your eye off the ball. Allow yourself to become too dispirited when things aren't going so well and you harm your own chances of them improving quickly. How you behave in one extreme affects your behaviour in the other extreme.

I suppose my reaction to winning trophies was considered a little odd, but it all played into that principle. Most players – at Everton and other clubs – celebrated raucously, and I totally understood why they did so. For them, winning a trophy was a concrete recognition of their hard work and what they'd achieved. It was why all the long hours were worth it.

But for me it was all a bit awkward. I was never happy receiving adoration or being the centre of attention. After we won the FA Cup Final in 1984, the first trophy of my senior career, I was overcome by a wave of embarrassment. I wanted to get my medal but didn't enjoy going up to the Royal Box, and I frankly found the lap of honour a bit much, even though I knew the supporters expected it.

I went to the post-match celebration at the Royal Lancaster Hotel. It wasn't my thing at all, and I rarely went to those events after we won trophies. But my parents had come down for the final and they really wanted to go, so of course I took them along. I would have been happier going back to the hotel and watching TV on the bed with a nice cup of tea. That was much more my thing.

I felt exactly the same in 1995, when we beat Manchester United in the final. I'd played really well in the match to stop United scoring, and in doing so I became the most decorated player in Everton's history. All of the players headed off to the party in the evening, but this time I felt no obligation to go.

My then wife Eryl and daughter Samantha had come down for the game, but they'd gone back home after the match and I had no interest in hanging around longer than I needed to. I drove home, got in at 10.30pm and went to bed. On the way home, I kept seeing cars full of Everton supporters driving back to Liverpool with smiles on their faces after winning the cup. That was all the recognition I ever needed, knowing that I had helped make every single one of them happy that day.

I also saw a car that had broken down by the side of the road, and the people standing by it had Manchester United shirts on. I stopped to pick them up and took them to a garage nearby. I'm sure the last thing that they expected was for Everton's goalkeeper to help them out on the evening of the final. It might have been different if we'd lost the game!

That wasn't to say that I didn't enjoy winning finals; of course I did. But the adoration I received for just doing my job always made me feel very awkward. If you go to work in any other field of employment and do the job to the best of your ability, nobody jumps around and celebrates and tells you that you're brilliant. We'd only done what we were supposed to do and knew we were capable of doing: winning.

My reaction was exactly the same when I won individual honours. It seemed odd for an individual player to be heralded in a team sport, when nothing would have been possible without the help of my teammates. I felt pretty uneasy to be given so many plaudits when the people around me had done so much of the work.

In a purely footballing context, confidence can be drained in a huge variety of ways but it will always be expressed on the pitch, because that's the main stage. So talk to players individually, sit down with them and get them to open up. Ask them if everything is all right at home, and if they're sleeping properly. There's no excuse anymore, with the rise in awareness of mental health issues and the use of sports psychologists. But I don't think managers always do it. Some are far too hands-off, and it sends the wrong message.

That's why you have to admire what Klopp has done – and what Kendall did before him. Everyone sees the great football that Klopp's team plays, and the shots of him hugging and smiling with the players, but he also prides himself on knowing each one of them inside out. They know that they can come to him with any problems, and he knows that he can give them constructive criticism without denting their confidence. It's a two-way street. So they're motivated to look after themselves off the pitch, work hard in training and prepare properly for matches. That's all down to maintaining their confidence.

Footballers express themselves more when they're confident, because *human beings* express themselves more when they're confident. And losing confidence means a lack of ability to be yourself, or a lack of faith in being yourself. That can be incredibly hard to deal with mentally.

Imagine a cross-dresser, a man whose family doesn't know about his cross-dressing. Let's say they all go out for a family lunch, and he's aware that his family might want to come back to his house afterwards. Imagine being worried about them finding female clothes and therefore needing to hide them. How would that lunch feel for this person, being constantly fearful about his relatives discovering something that he wasn't yet ready to share with them? Could he eat his food and enjoy the meal as normal, or would he have something in the back of his mind, nagging away? Now extend that to every day of his life.

It's exactly the same principle for a footballer. If you have any baggage or any doubts in your mind, it's more than likely that they'll affect you more on the pitch than elsewhere. Allow the situation to continue unaddressed, and careers and lives can be destroyed. Forget that a footballer is a human being, even for one minute, and you're leaving them open to mental health issues.

Confidence

by Anne-Marie Silbiger

In all of us lies the urge
to be confident
with our friends
lovers and strangers

2

PRESSURE

'Learn to push boundaries if it breaks down
walls, but when others dictate your actions
it's time to take ten steps back.'
Asha Iqbal, mental health activist and
honour-based violence survivor
(@_socialdrone)

What really is pressure? Is it a self-made construct, forged in your own mind? Is it entirely created by external factors? Or is it, as seems most likely, a bit of both?

Pressure will always exist for a player – the key lies in managing it. You can control the self-made pressure, and football clubs, managers and supporters can control the external pressures. Only by getting all of these groups pushing in the same direction can you effectively reduce it until it no longer affects performance. Contented players feel far less pressure than those who feel the weight of expectation pushing down on them. It's that simple.

Before an important, high-profile match it's inevitable that you become aware that you and the rest of the team are carrying people's expectations; you can't escape that. But on a normal day you go to the ground to not let yourself down,

then not let your family down, then not let the club down …
and only then not let the fans down. That's the natural order
for most players, I think. And knowing that natural order
allows you to reduce the pressure.

I used to say to myself, 'Well, what else do you want to do?'
And the answer was always, 'Nothing.' I wanted to play football, I knew I could be successful at it, and I used that as a
means of reducing the pressure on myself. On my debut for
Bury, I got booed by my own supporters. We were playing
against Wigan Athletic, and when I ran onto the pitch for the
warm-up they shouted, 'Fuck off, you're fucking shit.' I
remembered that incident for a long time. Most people there
trusted me, but there was a tiny minority who clearly didn't
like change and who already had their favourite goalkeeper.
They really didn't like the fact that I'd replaced John Forrest,
the previous No. 1.

I can understand that – they didn't know me and I was a
nobody. That might cause some young goalkeepers to freeze.
But honestly, I never let that stuff create any extra pressure on
me. I'd come to Bury to see if I could make it as a professional
footballer, and everything that happened from that point
onwards was me proving to myself and others that I could do it.

Next I went to Everton, and the pressure could have
increased at a bigger club in the First Division. But I reasoned
that the worst that could happen was that it didn't work out
and I went back to Bury or similar, and the best that could
happen was that I continued to prove that I could do it. And
I knew which I wanted.

Some games are bigger than others, but I just made them
part of the process too, because I wanted to play in those

matches. If you sat down and overanalysed it, then that pressure might get to you; so you had to avoid that. You simply had to walk over the white line and play the match.

I understand the notion of big-game pressure and how it affects certain people. But for me, the bigger the game, the better it was. When you get to a certain level and play against lower teams, you've got to be ruthless and show that you're better than them. But when you play against elite opponents, you just want to find out if you're better than them. And when you play against them and you do prove that you are, you just want to do it again and again.

There's also a need to compare your own situation with real-world pressures. I know that there are different types of pressure in the modern game with the money involved, that the players are expected to perform consistently and everything is televised. But real pressure is having no food in the house and the bailiffs knocking on the door. That has to put footballing pressure into some context.

Did I want to walk over that white line? Yes. Why did I want to walk over it? Because I enjoyed doing it and I knew that everyone in the stadium would cut their arm off to be in my position. That wasn't pressure, it was an honour. Did I have my health and little in my life to worry about? Yes. So I was fortunate. At that point, you realise that going out and having fun was the key. As long as I prepared to the best of my ability, there was nothing else I could do. That's a reason to remove pressure, not add it.

One of the best lessons I was ever taught about pressure was to laugh in the face of it. At Bury, the manager Jim Iley hired former Manchester United manager Wilf McGuinness as a coach, and he was absolutely brilliant with us. He was an excellent hands-on coach, but the best thing about Wilf was the way he could build your confidence with just a few words.

'When you get into the team, centre-forwards are going to try and smash you,' Wilf said to me. 'There's no reason for that, other than it's what they do to try and intimidate you. If you just get up and laugh, they won't know what's going through your head. Just get up and don't react. Just laugh at them.'

For goalkeepers, some situations can be intimidating, so you just have to rise above them. I remember playing Wimbledon in the FA Cup in 1993, and John Fashanu told me, 'The next time you challenge me it will be your last.' But again I just laughed it off. It was all part of his strategy to gain an advantage, and laughing at it was my strategy to do the same.

How much pressure you feel can also depend on your manager. Howard Kendall was the best manager I had at relieving it. When he was under serious heat at Everton during 1983/84, and close to the sack, he was brilliant at reducing the pressure on us. The training and team spirit were still good, but Liverpool were flying in the league and we were struggling to score goals, particularly at Goodison. Between the beginning of the season and the turn of the year, we'd played eleven league games at home and only scored seven times.

Howard came home after training one day and an Everton fan had spray-painted 'Kendall out' on the door of his garage. You saw other graffiti around the city with similar messages, and supporters were handing out leaflets outside home games demanding that the manager and chairman leave their posts.

But Howard never even mentioned the word 'pressure'. Nothing changed. Sometimes when you're under the cosh you can hear it in someone's voice, the frustration that what they believe in isn't working. With Howard, there was none of that. He was like a breeze. He would simply come in and stress the importance of enjoying ourselves. He was never one to harass the players to do better in a negative way, and he never shouted at us. Everything was just normal.

It's really difficult at times, when you're struggling, to make it a fun environment without looking like you aren't taking it seriously. When times are hard, negative people tend to panic and look too hard for solutions that aren't there. But Howard was able to trust his processes and trust his players. Of course, he occasionally tried new things on matchday and with team personnel, but he always stuck to his philosophy.

When things are going badly you expect change and upheaval. It's really difficult not to panic when you're personally under pressure. Everyone has their own way of dealing with it, but most people tend to get more stampy and aggressive. Howard was never like that. He believed that his methods and his philosophy could work, even if they took longer to succeed than most people thought they would.

The club was also good – that needs to be said. By keeping faith in Howard and being patient with him when things were going badly, it reduced the pressure on him, which in turn meant he didn't pass any stress on to us. There were calls from the media and supporters for the club to make a change, but the chairman ignored them and just let Howard get on with it. We came through it, and we got our rewards by the end of the season. Those rewards were the prize the club and manager deserved for their perseverance.

That's not to say that Howard wasn't afraid to experiment. I remember we once had a comedian come into the training ground to try to lift our spirits. But it wasn't so much what Howard did, as what he didn't do. He didn't rant and rave. He had answers for people who asked questions. The difference between him and Mike Walker was that Mike couldn't answer the questions; he just told the players that they weren't fit. With Howard, he'd always have thought about the potential questions that players and the media might ask, and he had serious, sensible answers for them.

We had a really good environment in the dressing room, and that has to help. Humour makes it easier. The dressing room is like an accident and emergency department, where you have cutting and dark humour – but you wouldn't take any of that outside. It's done to create an environment in which you can work effectively for the purposes of the job without focusing on the pressures on you to perform. If you're inside, everything is up for grabs. But if anyone attacks you from the outside, everyone has your back and you rally round.

I spent six months trying to please Howard, because every time I came in after playing well he'd say, 'Yes, but what about that kick or that throw-out?' It drove me wild, but it motivated me into thinking that the only way to shut him up was to be better still. Then one day I came in and he gave me a compliment. My self-belief shot through the roof and any pressure that might have built up just dropped away. Brian

Clough did the same with his players, because even a hand-shake from him would be enough to make them feel brilliant. It turned out that Howard knew me better than I knew myself.

Howard never said that you can't do this and you can't do that. If I wanted to do something, he let me do it – he trusted that I was always looking for ways to improve. But his management was proof that there are so many variables that can alter the pressure a player feels.

Over the summer of 1983, Howard had given all of his goalkeepers a chance to impress in pre-season matches. Jim Arnold and I had played a similar number of league matches the previous season, and I thought I had a good chance of being the No. 1 on the opening day. But when the team sheets were announced for the home game against Stoke City, Jim was in goal. With only one substitute allowed at the time, I had to watch the game from the stands.

But then I was very good at not letting things like that bother me. The biggest contradiction of my career was that I was motivated to the point of obsession about wanting to be in the team and play football, but if I wasn't selected I was very philosophical about it and rarely got angry or bitter. Although I could have believed that the work I'd put in over the summer had gone to waste because I still wasn't the first choice, that was never my thought process.

Instead, I reasoned that it was a message to tell me to work even harder and be even more focused on my own improve-ment. It was merely another challenge for me to overcome. The only way I could change the manager's decision was by proving that I was better than Jim. I couldn't change what had already happened; what will be, will be.

And it tended to work. On 1 October that first season, for an away game at Notts County, I was back in the team. I don't think Jim had really done anything wrong, and we'd only conceded seven goals in our opening seven matches, but Howard often made calls like that based on his gut instinct.

Maybe if I'd gone a whole season without ever making the team, despite my hard work, I might have got a little more disillusioned at the lack of games I was being given despite being confident in my own ability. But every time I was left out of the team or suffered a setback, working doubly hard seemed like both the obvious response and the one most likely to succeed.

I think as a goalkeeper, the pressure on you is slightly separated from the team, and that probably allowed me to cope more easily. But it works the other way too. I played really well out in Holland in 1996 in a World Cup qualifier, when Wales lost 7–1. I had probably the best game of my career and honestly could have conceded twenty times. But despite being content with my performance, I couldn't be outwardly happy because the team had been humiliated.

Although I could move on from mistakes, in the aftermath of them happening I'd be furious with myself. If I was on the way home from a match in which I'd made a mistake for a goal but we'd won, I could have run someone over. That's an awful thing to say, but it's true. It would take me until the following Monday to get over it and shut it away, even though I knew it was a stupid reaction. For me, it was the embarrassment of letting people down.

In those situations too, humour helps. I'd go into training on a Monday morning after conceding a goal or two at the weekend and the players would take the piss out of me – 'You were shite on Saturday, Nev.' OK, fair enough, I was. But then it was over. And if supporters or journalists ever gave me grief, then my teammates would defend me to the hilt. It's when they weren't taking the piss that you knew you had a real problem.

The toughest period was between getting home on the Saturday night and the Monday after a mistake, because you were frustrated and separated from the game. That frustration depended upon the result of the match, how the rest of the game went and who was in charge. Sometimes if we lost, you could reason that the manager had picked the wrong team, played the wrong system or made the wrong substitutions. But you learnt to quickly put it away, otherwise you'd only risk it leading to more frustration.

Yet being the goalkeeper meant that I felt impervious to the pressure that the manager and the rest of the team were probably feeling. Perhaps that wasn't right. Maybe I should have been trying to gee everyone up more. But I was selfish, and I believed that being selfish was the only way that I could be successful. Being obsessed with my own preparation and my own performance was my main strategy for getting the best out of myself, and I figured that if the team weren't playing well then that only made my own performance level more crucial.

Sometimes I didn't care if the team all played badly together. Because if that happened, then the chances were that we weren't a bad team, we'd just had an off day or the system wasn't right – and these things can be addressed. The worst was if four or five first-team players were regularly having off days, because that increased the pressure on your own performance through no fault of your own.

As a goalkeeper, you aren't really in control of how the team plays. You can obviously make a difference with your own saves – by giving your defenders confidence – and with your distribution, but that only goes so far. You can't make things happen further up the pitch, and if you concentrate on trying to then you'll probably make things worse, not better.

I couldn't make the strikers score, but I could save shots and make sure that the worst we got was a 0–0 draw. And if the players in front of me knew that I was doing everything I could to keep a clean sheet, it reassured them because it took some of the pressure off. That sort of thing made a difference, even if it might have come from my own selfishness.

In our first thirteen games of 1984, we only conceded six goals. The strikers found their form too, and we set off on an unbeaten streak, winning eight times. From being booed by our own fans and Howard getting personal abuse, we relieved all the pressure on ourselves in the league – eventually finishing seventh – and went on a run in the cup competitions that eventually ended with us beating Watford at Wembley. I conceded one solitary goal in the entire FA Cup run.

For players nowadays, there's obviously more cameras around, and everyone has a phone with a camera and will post pictures on social media. That leads to players feeling increasingly restricted in what they do and what they say, which threatens to create a claustrophobia and loneliness that ramps up the pressure you feel.

Everyone wants to see more characters in the modern game and bemoans the lack of individuality in the personalities of players, but it's tricky because as soon as someone raises their head above the parapet they get hammered from a different section of the public or the media. Paul Gascoigne is the perfect example of that, with people leaving bottles of beer outside his house so that they can get a picture of him. Now that's really sad, because it doesn't help him.

I think everyone in the public eye has a shelf-life of being the one in the media spotlight, and therefore in the public's consciousness too. That's a really unpleasant reality, because it must be damaging to the mental health of those people who suffer the cycle of being built up and knocked down, and – because the focus is on a select, chosen few – also affects the confidence of top players who aren't heralded at all.

When I was in good form but had an off day, I'd come home knowing that I'd played like shit. But I might look in the newspaper and read that I'd got 'unlucky' for the goal. That word was only used because the media liked me at the time, so they judged me by different rules than other goalkeepers. As footballers, when you're young you get the benefit of the doubt because you have potential. Then you've got a long middle section, followed by a point at which you're judged to be over the hill.

Now your performance level might not change much over your whole career, but the way in which you're perceived does change. What once might have been considered to be 'unlucky' is later viewed as 'clumsy' or evidence that you're 'in decline'. You might have been be lauded for having a personality and some character, but that can be warped into you being a troublemaker or a loose cannon. And all this seems to be led by the media.

We've seen it time and time again with young English players, especially with Gazza. The media delighted in his antics because he was both brilliant at football and did foolish things that sold copies. He was the media's hero until he was no longer at his peak and he wasn't considered of use to them. They then removed that golden boy status and exploited his problems for their own gain. Just imagine how damaging that process is to someone's mental health.

Gazza should have been working in a school like ours. Kids would have loved him to bits, because he has the sort of innocence and enthusiasm that would have made him connect with them. He loved to entertain as a player, and loved the idea that young kids were watching him and became inspired to play football by his example. He could have had exactly the same impact after playing, and it would have helped him mentally to cope with life without football.

It was the lack of football in his life that allowed Gascoigne's problems to take hold; he had no structure without the game. But with that structure and with proper friends, not those who were out to play on his fame and exploit his wealth, he'd have been far better off. He should have been given a role working with youth teams and then out in the community interacting with kids through football, and he would have made a huge difference to so many lives because he has that innate ability to connect. Doing this would have given him a greater purpose in life.

Instead, he lost his structure and then suffered at the hands of a tabloid media that turned his struggles with addiction into front-page news to sell papers. At no point in that process did they ever reach out to him and offer help. He became their property without him asking for it.

Gazza is a high-profile and extreme example of someone who suffered without structure, but there are many others who have struggled with the same issue. It's no different to normal life. If you've worked in a factory for thirty-five years, and one day you come in and, without warning, learn that it's been shut down, then your purpose to get up in the morning has been ripped from you. How do you replace that? How do you cope?

Anybody that becomes popular will one day become unpopular, or at best ignored. Your face is in the newspaper or on TV every day, and then suddenly ... nothing. That's either because you've become so ubiquitous that the media needs a new version of you to take your place, or needs to give a different – most probably negative – side of you to maintain your notoriety. And there's a constant conveyor belt of people who will take your place. Popularity has a shelf-life.

For whatever reason, the media paints certain people in a certain way and deliberately skates over elements of their lives or personalities that don't fit the image they want to portray. Take George Michael, when he was alive. The amount of charity work George did was extraordinary, but the media focus only ever seemed to be on his sexuality and private life. It's the same with Elton John, who has done some astonishing work with AIDS charities. But that's never the focus.

The key is to avoid being swayed by either extreme. Don't get carried away by the praise and buy into the notion that you're some kind of national treasure, and in the same way don't take any notice when they cast you aside. But to be fair, it's so much easier said than done, because it happens to young, impressionable people, and it can be heart-warming to read complimentary things about yourself. The problem is that this persuades you to emotionally invest in the opinions of these people, which then sets you up for the fall.

My agent would always tell me not to worry about what the papers said. They didn't know me as well as I knew myself, so it didn't matter if they said I'd played well or played badly, just as long as I could judge myself how I'd played. And whatever they wrote became fish and chip paper the following day anyway. I never really set my stall on what anyone said if I didn't know them or respect them as an expert on me or goalkeeping.

But for some people it does make a massive difference, because their careers become defined by how often they're on the front page of newspapers, and so the nature of the coverage creates a huge pressure on them. I honestly don't know how that type of celebrity copes, and I know that plenty don't. Popularity is a very odd concept, but you have to remember that nothing about you needs to change to meet the supposed standards they set for you. If they like you, fine. If they don't like you, fine. If you want to change, fine. But you have to stay true to yourself, not some version of you that they've constructed.

It's easy to see why the English media and English fans hype up young English footballers. What they're doing is selling a dream. They're not just hyping you up, they're pushing the idea that you could be the answer for the country and will finally take England back to where they think the team belongs. Then when you inevitably fail to live up to that unrealistic hype, you get flak.

Take Tom Davies at Everton. He comes into the team at the age of eighteen and tries his bollocks off, so everyone says, 'Oh, he gets it, he's a breath of fresh air, he's the future.' Then when he suffers a period of patchy form, like every young player does, or the team isn't performing so well, it's, 'He's shit, get him out of the team.' By the age of twenty-one he's already gone through that entire cycle and now has to move on. Judge Tom Davies on the situation he was put into, the lack of help he got from senior pros in the team, the changing managers, the fact that he's a bloody kid.

How hard is that for him to deal with? He's still learning and developing as a player and person, but now he has so much piled on top of him and he's having to do it all in the public eye. How strong do you have to be to manage that and come out level-headed the other side?

It can be enough to break a kid. They might start to shy away from the ball, scared of the criticism that they'll face if they make a mistake. They might play it safe, which is against their natural instincts and so reduces them as a player. They might go and mark someone when they don't have the ball so they don't get given it. And to top it all, they'll get groaned at by 40,000 people if it goes wrong. But supporters don't seem to care. They just think, 'Oh well, we can just go out and buy someone for £40 million anyway.'

That's the horrible side of football. The money isn't good, the inequality is bad too. But the lack of patience and the lack of senior professionals helping out younger kids on the pitch and making things easier for them is awful. That's cheating. That's not doing your job.

Managers are more fearful for their jobs than they've ever been, and that pressure will always be passed down to the players. Nowadays, I don't think that a manager should have to do anything other than organising the first team. The club should have an identity, and everyone should know what that identity is. The academy should produce players to match the identity of the club and its philosophy. And then you pick the manager to fit that philosophy.

But they don't. Despite managers having more pressure on them, we've actually given them more to do and less time in which to do it. Clubs lurch between one philosophy and the next. One manager gets sacked, another comes in – and everything shifts. They have to say, 'We are this club and this is how we do things.' The philosophy should be set in stone and everything should be built around that.

You look at West Ham: from Slaven Bilić to David Moyes to Manuel Pellegrini and back to Moyes again. Where is the philosophy there? At Everton, Sam Allardyce came in – but it was never going to work because certain managers just don't fit at certain places. For a while there's been something fundamentally wrong at Manchester United, where supposedly world-class players won't – or don't – perform. But is there a philosophy that everyone is working within?

I also think that there are managers who can spend money, and managers who aren't suited to it. There's managers like José Mourinho, and that is – or maybe was – his thing. Collecting expensive players and managing them and their personalities. Then there are others who prefer working-class English lads who graft, and that's their thing.

You take Moyes and Allardyce. Look at the type of players they were and the type of people they are. And they have managed players who haven't tried a leg. Are they allowed to tell the truth to them? Can they inspire them? But if everything is geared towards creating a certain type of player, managers can walk into the job with their eyes open – and the club have appointed them because of it. They have a mandate. Then they can be the best managers they can be. It all goes back to being the best of you, not a version of someone else.

If your club is constantly changing managers and lurching between philosophies, and each manager that comes in has different ideas and one might like you and another might not, that's very hard for players. You're increasing the pressure on them when you should be easing it.

So don't expect managers to build the club when you haven't already created an environment in which they're able to do so. Tell them to manage the first team to play in a certain style, and ensure that any player who comes in fits with that philosophy. Because when you walk into the canteen at the training ground, you can instantly spot the mood and tell whether everything is or isn't going to be perfect on the pitch.

There's a really interesting point about reducing pressure that comes from American sport and the psychology of that country. There, the typical scenario is that everybody is incredibly upbeat and positive and 'Have a nice day!'. This extends to sport, where everything is presented as a positive, every mistake is an opportunity, and they try to engineer a spirit where every supporter coming to the match believes wholeheartedly in the team winning. In this country, we some-times see that constant positivity as ugly or brash, as if confi-dence and cheerfulness were something to be sheepish or embarrassed about. But I want everyone coming to the stadium to believe wholeheartedly that we can win. And you'd be amazed at the difference that can make.

There are some brilliant psychologists now working at the biggest clubs in the world, but clubs don't do anything with the crowd other than making them pay more and more for the same tickets. Why don't they work with them? There are 40,000 people there that you can use to your advantage to reduce the pressure on your own players and increase the pressure on your opponents.

Concentrate on the grounds and the crowds. Get those people wound up to back their team. Get them to make some noise. Make sure that everyone is up for a good time. If you do – whatever happens in the match – they *will* have a good time. Don't assume that the fans will come whatever, and don't make them pay ludicrous prices for a shit burger and the same seat. Every matchday has to be an event. We seem to be scared in this country of letting people enjoy themselves.

The clubs don't help. They effectively make it clear that they can do whatever they want and the supporters will come anyway, so they don't need to try. So go the other way. Look at everything: the music, the colour schemes, fan involvement. Don't just plasticise everything or roll it in glitter. Maximise the experience for supporters by giving them things that they really need. If it's raining or cold, give them hot drinks or hand out umbrellas at the transport hubs. Or even, and I know this is completely alien to them, reduce ticket prices. I think Leicester City winning the league is a really good example of this. It wasn't just that the team had a great shared morale, but that every supporter believed that the owner cared.

If every club did that, the supporters would think, 'Bloody hell, this club values me, they've thought about me, so now I'm going to do everything I can to cheer them on, rather than sitting back and waiting to be entertained and shouting criticism at the players when they fail to entertain me.'

Then there's the players on matchday. The interesting thing to me is that the players are all fit, but some of them are deemed unable to last ninety minutes. Is that because the game is more intense and more demanding? Perhaps. But is it also because we've created an environment in which players are psychologically programmed to break down, because they've been left unprepared for obstacles in the road by the lack of expression allowed in their personal lives? Maybe this also makes it harder for them to express themselves on the pitch. Perhaps this creates a pressured scenario in which players feel that everything matters so much now that they become tense, too tense. When they get the ball and when they walk down the street, are they allowed to be themselves?

There's a danger that such an environment leads to a culture of fear, which creates its own pressure. If I know that I can't give the ball away because the opposition might score, the manager might get sacked because he becomes impatient with the club philosophy and I might get crucified on social media, then it's going to be very difficult to play with any freedom. That pushes players into their shells, so they play it safe and try not to lose or, worse, try to stay hidden.

But for whatever reason – and it's probably pure greed – clubs fail to make the connection between looking after the supporters and reducing the pressure on players. They chase money as much as they can and forget to create a positive environment – then they wonder why their players feel unable to express themselves under the extra pressure they have piled onto them.

Pressure

by Anne-Marie Silbiger

Some of us are delinquents in hiding
No call to achieve
Yet the demand to be somebody
Looms thunderous in those ears

3

FEAR

'Ten seconds of fear can change your life forever.'
Elizabeth Gregory, clinical psychologist
(@DizzyDoodler)

I managed to avoid the pitfalls of fear during my career, for the most part. I think this was partly because of my mental strength, most of which came naturally, and partly preparation. To take just one example: I could have feared serious injury – but then I can't control that and I'm more likely to get injured if I'm worrying about it anyway.

I also used to try to look for the positive in everything. So I'm playing Liverpool today. Everyone in the ground would love to be me here, so I should do all I can do to make the most of it – and that means banishing fear.

Some players might look at that situation and be scared, because of the pressure it was going to impose on their performance. But I saw it totally differently. Even if I went out and had the worst game in the world, all the 40,000 people there would still love to be me. So who am I to throw this away, when it's something that I've always wanted to do and I'm half-decent at it? That guy in the crowd standing there screaming shit at me would go and get changed in an instant to come on and play. But it's me who's got this chance – you can't buy it and you can only earn it. All of these people are living their dreams partly through me.

On the way to the ground on the coach, the build-up would begin – you'd see people around you getting twitchy and their nerves beginning to show. But what was the worst-case scenario? That I don't play well. But I can't possibly play well every week, so what's to fear? That sounds simple, but it's how I felt.

What more could I ask for than being a footballer? I play for ninety minutes and go home – happy days. I was good at it, but I worked bloody hard at it. If you worked hard all week to get better and you prepared properly, the match was the best time, not the worst. And if somebody was destined to have a better day than me, then so be it.

I think there's something very positive about going with your gut feeling. Sometimes now, I'll have to go to places that I'm not hugely comfortable with – perhaps I'm making a speech, and I hate using scripts. I have to just get up and talk, sometimes with little idea other than the general theme. But that way you avoid lecturing people or becoming set in a certain way of doing things; you find it easier to adapt to the moment. You're also more likely to dig into your feelings and let people see your emotion for the subject. Football was the same.

I just think, 'Right, if this speech goes shit, what's the worst that can happen?' Am I still OK? Yes. Does it matter if some people think I'm a knob? Plenty probably think that anyway. If I can do it and it goes well, great. But if it doesn't, what can I do about it then? All of these responses are reasons to banish fear rather than allow it to build up.

You also have to remember that players – and people – are always their own worst critics. I have come out of speeches, gone home, got into bed and Emma has asked how it went. I've said it was shit and that I was shit, and then the next day spoke to the fella who organised the event and he's said that everybody loved it. So you always need to keep as much perspective as possible.

Nothing about the game ever frightened me. I reasoned that I had a simple choice. There's the tunnel. You either go down that tunnel and find out something new about yourself (and, yes, sometimes that might not be a positive experience), or you go home and never play again. I always wanted to find out about myself and discover whether I could succeed in new challenges, and I'm very fortunate that I was built that way.

There's a period when you go to a new job when everything is unfamiliar, and so it feels strange and unsettling. The interview is weird, because nobody talks in an interview like they talk in the real world or on the job. They ask you questions like, 'Name three of your biggest weaknesses.' Those first few days can be really hard, and that's what going out onto the pitch can be like early in your career or at a new club, but the reason you went for the interview is because you wanted the job. So you go in and give it your best shot. Soon it becomes easier, and eventually you can't even imagine why you were worried in the first place.

I think my fearless attitude was partly learnt through the circumstances of my early career. I started playing men's football at the age of twelve. That wasn't really through choice, more being asked to and not being brave enough to say no. When you're older you might learn to make choices, but at twelve – and desperate to play any football – you just take orders. Those matches taught me that being fearful was one way to make things harder for myself than they already were.

'Fear' – that uncontrollable, unmoving, debilitating emotion – is the wrong word for whatever I felt. I was apprehensive, perhaps. But it's like going into battle, albeit with far less serious consequences. If you sat down beforehand and thought about everything that could or might go wrong, you'd scare yourself shitless. You know that you aren't going to refuse to play, so it becomes a process of emotionally preparing to block out any potentially negative thoughts. Then you get used to it day by day, because you get desensitised to what you're about to do. Your mind and body learn to cope.

It's actually sometimes the flipside that becomes the bigger problem. You begin to become so desensitised to the pressure and the importance of the match that you start not being affected by nerves at all, and that's when complacency can creep in. In that sense, fear can be used as a positive. It can be utilised as a motivational tool to prepare yourself properly.

I do also believe in things happening for a reason and in the presence of fate. That's probably a coping mechanism, because it takes things out of my control and so allows me to process them more easily. All I can do is prepare the best I can, do the best I can and then the rest is down to fate. If you're having a bad time, you reason that it's because you've done really well until that point and so fate has intervened to remind you why it matters so much. If I ever got a bad injury, that was fate reminding me to look after myself the best I could and make sure I didn't pick up any more unnecessary injuries.

But you have to do everything in your power to get fate on your side. Some people who believe in fate might use it as an excuse to not try their hardest at something because fate may go against them anyway, but I've always firmly believed that what you get out of something is directly related to what you put in.

It's very rare that I go to do something and it doesn't lead to something else, whether it's a contact I'm given by reaching out through Twitter, or someone I meet at a conference from a mental health charity who introduces me to some great ideas. By putting in the miles and the hours, you make things happen for yourself.

Your job, whether it's campaigning for mental health or playing football, is to minimise the impact of fate by taking control of situations. There are things that I haven't particularly wanted to do, but you do them through your faith that your perseverance will pay off and that fate will determine that you're rewarded for it.

Arrogance is often mis-sold as a negative, but it can be a really useful thing for a footballer to help reduce their fear. In fact, I think you need a certain arrogance as a player because it maintains your self-belief, creating a shell around you that enables you to deflect not just doubt but also criticism. Maintain that shell, and high performance becomes self-fulfilling: 'I've proved that I'm better than my opposition before, so – if I prepare properly – I'll do it again.' I used to play against the Dutch national team in the 1980s, and they all knew just how good they were. They had a swagger that said, 'We're better than you and we're very happy to prove it.'

So I don't mind anyone who's arrogant, if they back it up with their performances. What I can't stand is people who come across as arrogant and yet they fail to deliver on it. Misplaced arrogance is as damaging as a lack of confidence. It means that you aren't self-analysing, and you're taking your eye off the ball about what really matters. You're making it about you as a personality, not you as a footballer.

There's a massive difference between thinking that you're very good and knowing how good you are. Look at Rolls-Royce. They don't advertise on TV, because they don't need to. They know how exclusive they are and they know that everyone realises the quality of their product. But if they thought, 'We don't need to advertise,' and started getting slap-dash with their new models, people wouldn't buy them.

As a footballer, you require a level of arrogance because you need to go out there and perform with the total belief that you'll deliver. I love going to the theatre, because there's something fascinating about watching actors put themselves out there night after night. You can tell the hard work that's gone into it beforehand. Those actors need to have something within them that says 'I belong here' and allows them to puff out their chests, go onto the stage and show off. But if they got all their lines wrong, you'd wonder why they were so confident.

I went out at the old Wembley Stadium for the FA Cup Final in 1984 in front of 100,000 people and millions more watching on TV, and I needed to be able to say 'I'm good enough to cope with this' and believe it too. That requires a certain amount of ego or arrogance, otherwise you'd risk crumbling to pieces.

Here's an example of arrogance working for a goalkeeper. I was taking a coaching session as part of doing my goalkeeping badges, and I said to them that the best thing you can do when a striker is through on goal is to get yourself into a good position away from goal and then stay completely still.

Whose job is it to score? The striker probably gets paid more money than you, and everyone expects the striker to score when through on the keeper. The pressure is all on them. So why would you make it easier for them? By moving one way or the other, you're helping to make their decision for them, and they're waiting for you to make that mistake and make it easy for them.

Now in those moments, staying still is often the hardest thing to do. Inaction can be braver than action, and you feel under pressure to make your move. But by having a total belief in your ability – that sense of arrogance – you're saying to them, 'I'm not moving anywhere, mate. This one's on you. I'm not scared of you.'

The number of times that a striker in that situation ends up shooting straight at the goalkeeper is fascinating. Everyone criticises the striker for missing the chance, and you can see why, but they missed because they waited so long for you to show them where to shoot that they ended up panicking and rushing it. It's a game of chicken, and your lack of fear owned the situation.

But you don't need to go around shouting about how good you are. Arrogance should be an internal emotion. Your actions should speak for you. I find it hard sometimes when I look at players who act like they've taken on the world and won, and they haven't even achieved half of what they can. It's one thing acting like that when you're Cristiano Ronaldo, but another entirely when you're doing it having finished outside the top four.

One inevitable reason for fear as a footballer is the possibility of your status within the first-team squad being diminished, or a manager losing confidence in you. It's obviously never a good sign for a goalkeeper if the manager is actively looking to buy another keeper. There's only one of you in the team, so any purchase in the pipeline suggests that he has doubts about your ability.

Also, when a manager buys a player he automatically becomes more loyal to them. They become his property because they pushed for the signing. They're more likely to get into the team than existing players, because if they don't then the chairman starts asking why the player was signed.

In the summer of 1996 I knew that Joe Royle was interested in buying another goalkeeper. I thought he might look for a younger player to give me some competition, but also as cover for me. But then Howard told me that he was trying to sign Nigel Martyn from Crystal Palace. Nigel was a fair bit younger than me but he was first choice at Palace, so it was unlikely that he'd sign just to sit on the bench.

Understandably, the media were saying that this might be the end of my Everton career. You could see their point – I was thirty-seven at the time. But I went to see the manager and told him that I didn't care if he did sign Nigel, because I still thought I was better than him and was happy to prove it.

I can't say I was fearful of Nigel coming, although he eventually joined Leeds anyway. It would certainly have provided me with an extra challenge and I might have been fighting against the manager's new favourite. But life is a series of challenges, and sometimes they provoke the best in you to come out.

The main cause of fear, however, and it's something that's forever at the back of players' minds to a greater or lesser extent, is serious injury. Your entire career, your professional life, can be ripped away in one single moment. Injury is an inevitable part of a footballer's lot, and it can be worse for a goalkeeper. People say that goalkeepers have to be fearless because you're expected to put your head and body where other players put their boots. But to me it was always instinctive. If you have to think about whether to do something like that, then you probably aren't going to be a top goalkeeper. Just entertaining the thought indicates an element of doubt.

Being a goalkeeper is like being a boxer – it's not whether you'll get hurt or not, it's about how you deal with pain when you do, and learning to embrace it as part of the job. You also have to be prepared to hurt other people. I remember punching Graham Stuart in the face when he was playing for Chelsea and I came for a cross. It wasn't deliberate, but some players might dwell on moments like that and let them shape their future behaviour. If you hurt someone badly in an accidental challenge then it clearly isn't pleasant, but you have to treat it as part and parcel of the game.

When you come back from a serious injury, it feels like the beginning of your career all over again – the feelings and thoughts you have are just the same. You've got the trepidation about coming into a settled team, about making sure not to let your teammates down and about trying to avoid any mistakes. You also know that a relapse of the injury could put your whole career in jeopardy. When the same injury happens in the same place twice and a flaw is exposed, you fear that permanent damage has been caused that will always exist as a weakness.

I think that coming back from serious injury was the time in my career when I was the most nervous. It was a step into the unknown, which was a strange, weird place for someone who liked to prepare for everything. But I didn't consider it scary as such, because I'd prepared in the gym and had encountered no problems there.

The worst injury of my career came towards the end of 1985/86, when Everton were pipped to the title by Liverpool in the final few weeks of the season. I was playing for Wales against Ireland at Lansdowne Road in late March, and the pitch was a mud bath because it had recently been used for Ireland's rugby matches. I went up for an aerial challenge, caught the ball and my foot landed in a hole in the pitch.

I dislocated my ankle and tore all the ligaments, with my foot pointing in the wrong direction. They took me to hospital, where I was given an anaesthetic, my ankle was popped back into place and I was told that I could be out for a year. I was the worst patient imaginable. John Clinkard, Everton's physio, had been told by the club doctor that I should avoid any exercise for a few months to allow the ligaments to heal, but I hated summer anyway and the thought of starting it three months early filled me with dread. I'd get Eryl – my ex-wife – to take me to the training ground, where I could do gym work and keep training my good leg. Even when John allowed me to do some sessions with him, I'd always go in early and do extra work on the indoor AstroTurf pitch without him knowing. It's genuinely a wonder that John didn't punch me, but he was brilliant for my recovery and I think he knew that there was no point trying to stop me.

When I came back from the injury in late October – ahead of schedule – my ankle still hadn't been seriously tested in training because it's basically impossible to replicate the conditions encountered in an actual match. You can't really expect your teammates to go in as hard in training; it just doesn't work like that.

I made my return against Watford, and there was a one-on-one incident – a 50/50 situation – where I ran out of goal to meet Mark Falco, the Watford striker. I won the ball, and his boot smashed into my ankle at exactly the place I'd suffered the original injury. I held my breath for a moment, waiting for a jolt of pain that never came. At that instant, I knew I'd healed properly.

It was probably the best thing that could have happened to me. We won the game, it was hard-fought and I'd had the ankle tested in a way I'd been unable to do before coming back. Until that test, I'd have had a doubt in the back of my mind about whether it was strong enough – and I'd have been waiting for a challenge exactly like Falco's. That doubt, however small, can affect your performance.

I think I'm pretty good at accepting things, and always have been. I get injured – so what? That's just life testing my resolve and my hunger to come back better and show the team exactly what they've missed. If we get to the ground late because we're stuck in traffic, so be it. It wasn't deliberate, there's nothing we could have done and there's nothing we can do about it now. So we deal with what we have. The alternative is to dwell on it, and in doing so let it ruin things in the future that we *can* control.

I learnt a lot from Jim Arnold, who was a goalkeeper at Everton when I signed. He got a groin strain but wanted to get fit, so he did nothing for the entire week and was passed fit for the Saturday, when he played really well. I was amazed at the mental strength that it took for him to avoid doing anything all week, when he was itching to train, and then be able to play that well at the weekend.

I was totally different. After two days being injured, I'd be going mad. Me and another physio nearly had a fight because I was always pushing to do more and more and test the injury out. I was an awful patient at the start of my career, going stir crazy. But Jim taught me to see things differently, to rest for good reason and trust the healing process.

That adaptability, a willingness to change my attitude towards things, was something I learnt along the way. I think a lot of it came from my grounding in the game, and where I played as a kid. When I think about the various methods of transport we used to have to take to get to matches, the various types of pitches we had to play on, the balls we had to use and the wide variety of teams we played, it's clear that it taught me to be adaptable and mentally prepare for last-minute problems.

If I'd been brought up in a modern academy, and everything was organised for me, I'm not sure if I'd have developed like that. I think there's far less scope for individual thought when you come through a Premier League academy. Everything has got to be just so. But the best solutions are the ones that you come up with yourself. Solving problems on your own demonstrates that you've got the analytical tools and also are able to self-analyse. It proves that you're mature enough to admit your own flaws, and more able to find solutions to them.

This all plays back into fear. If you've lived and worked in an academy system, and signed a contract worth £10 million, what's the worst that can happen? But if you're then in a situation for which you haven't been prepared and you haven't learnt to be adaptable, how could you not be fearful? I only lacked fear because I was certain that my development and upbringing had prepared me for every scenario as best as possible.

If a player isn't given a rounded picture of life, then they don't become rounded footballers or people. To reach your full potential you have to be you. But if you don't know yourself completely, how can you be?

Fear

by Anne-Marie Silbiger

Fear fixes us
It anchors feet to ground
Fear knows not of adventure
Or realising dreams

4

ABUSE

'It took me years to walk away with the scars
left by others but it's a constant reminder
of what I overcame.'

Asha Iqbal, mental health activist and
honour-based violence survivor
(@_socialdrone)

I didn't ever mind the crowd, and the more the better. What were they going to do – it's only words? And if they were shouting at me, and I knew I was able to cope with it and feed off it, then at least they wouldn't be shouting at one of my teammates, who perhaps would have been unable to react the same way.

If I was doing what I was supposed to be doing, then I honestly didn't hear much abuse from the stands anyway, although it obviously went on. A goalkeeper stands closer than any other player in the team to the stands – and has to stay there – so will always be a target for those in the crowd who want to scream and shout. I just used to try to block it out. I never read the newspapers to hear what people thought about me there, so I didn't really have much contact with criticism at all. I found that a very healthy stance to take.

The more people there were at a game, the less I heard any fans shouting because it just became a wall of noise. If you're having a bad time and there are 10,000 people or fewer at the game, then you can hear everything – and that's hard for some people to take. But you've got to endure these things, and you can't change what anyone in the crowd thinks other than by proving them wrong.

Sometimes I was able to use vile abuse as motivation, so rather than making life harder it would actually make it easier. Say we were playing at Old Trafford, and for whatever reason I didn't quite feel up for it. I'd walk over to the Stretford End in the warm-up, go right in front of the crowd and pretend to look at the pitch. I wasn't really, but I could be sure that it would provoke a series of shouts from the stands, and I'd use that abuse as motivational fuel. That's why I always liked playing away at Manchester United and Liverpool.

By showing absolutely no reaction in front of the Stretford End or the Kop, I was proving to both sets of fans that I held all the power and that they had no way of getting it off me. It became funny. You're all spending your time hurling abuse at me, but you're wasting your time because I'm just laughing. And then at the end of the game, if we'd won, I could walk off the pitch and wave to them. It never needed to be disrespectful and nasty. I used to get a lot of stick at Elland Road, but I never went anywhere where I thought, 'Bloody hell, that was so intimidating that it put me off my game.'

As a footballer you're always bound to get stick, but what are the fans so worried about? If they're taking time out from cheering on their club to shout at me, they must be concerned about what I can do. It's a compliment to you if people are trying to put you off your game. I remember a cup game Everton played at Bournemouth in 1985, not long after Wales had lost in World Cup qualifying. A section of Bournemouth's support was taunting me about not going to the World Cup. But I used that as a reason to show them how good I was and to ensure their team would go no further in the competition. We won the game 2–0.

I didn't really find any of the famously intimidating grounds to play at particularly daunting. In 1990 we played away at Millwall, but my ex-wife had chickenpox so I stayed behind to look after her and travelled down later than the team. I got to London by car, went to a cafe near the ground, had a bacon sandwich and a cup of tea, we won 2–1 and I played well. It's weird, but as a footballer things like that stick with you and define your whole impression of a place. I'd never be intimidated if we went there again, because I associated it with dashing to and from home and that relaxing pre-match routine.

Wales played against Spain in World Cup qualifying in 1984, and their home crowd started throwing oranges and snowballs at us while we warmed up. We picked them up, threw them back and turned it into a game. The Spanish police went berserk at us, and angrily told us to stop it. So we said, 'We will, when they stop throwing them at us!' But it was all a bit of fun.

Clearly, it's a little different when that abuse comes from your own supporters. At the start of 1994/95 I got some stick from Evertonians for my form. Someone at Goodison shouted that I was 'fucking shit' – and I heard it. I shouted back, 'Well, you can fuck off, you wanker' back at him. It all got blown up in the media and I got in trouble with the club, which seemed a bit harsh given that the fella had abused me first. But I was being disrespectful.

Shortly after that – related to the same incident, I think – I received a death threat through the post. It was threatening me with all sorts of things, and the fact that it came to my home address obviously scared me. You never want to think that your family might be put into any danger.

I went to the chairman, and he said fuck-all. I was incredibly disappointed with that at the time, because he just dealt with it like it was a regular occurrence. How many death threats are players getting if you're reacting like this? Well, it was my first one, so you can understand why I might be a little worried. But it all died down and never happened again.

At some point in your career you're going to get stick from the supporters. You can't be perfect, and they have frustrations because they pay their money and expect success. That's just how it is. If I walked out the ground and got substantial verbal abuse, I'd often reply to them – and they never expected that. In that moment they realise that you're just a normal human being like them. But I tried to let it wash over me. It was just pent-up frustration on their part, and they had an easy target in front of them to shout at.

Some players did get affected by it, and some got it far worse than me. When David Johnson came to Everton from Liverpool in 1982, having previously left Everton and gone on to join Liverpool, the fans absolutely hammered him. It was horrendous. Every time his name was mentioned over the Tannoy he'd be relentlessly booed. He had some bloody nerve, because despite all the abuse he carried on through it.

The Goodison crowd have always been fair, but the one thing they see through is frauds. If they think that someone doesn't care or isn't trying, they hate it – and they're happy to let you know. If you try and you're shit, they might occasionally tell you you're shit, but they appreciate the effort. Over the last decade they have taken against a few players because they believe that they don't care about the club. Goodison expects blood and thunder as a minimum.

I understand that. They're at the end of their working week. They're knackered. They're on the ale. They're paying a significant amount of money to watch a team that they're proud to call theirs, and they want to see evidence from highly paid players that they at least care. For supporters, football is about eternal hope. They'll continue to support because of that hope through thick and thin, but you can only take the piss out of them for so long – and then they'll break. And because they're not going to stop coming, they'll shout and scream instead.

But there's a difference between criticism and abuse. Everyone's going to get criticism, because nobody's perfect, yet no one deserves abuse. The first thing I'd think is whether the criticism is justified – have they got a point? Second, is this someone coming from a position of expertise or experience – should I be listening to them?

Once you work through these questions, you can deal with it. There's no point not taking what's said on board just because it offends you or you disagree with it. If you believe that they might have a point, even if you disagree with it and even if it wasn't expressed in the right way, it might still be worth processing it and working out if it should spark a change in behaviour or a new focus on a certain area.

If you process it fully, which takes some honesty, and you still think you're doing the right things and that the criticism was misplaced, you stick to your guns. But you have to go through that process to be able to make that call. It's exactly the same as someone giving you advice. What suits someone else might not suit you, but that doesn't mean that you don't listen to the advice. Never dismiss anything out of hand.

For players that are on social media, abuse has become an everyday occurrence. That's something I didn't have to deal with as a player. Apart from the death threat I received, once I was in the privacy of my own home I could shut myself away from any abuse or criticism. I had my four walls, and nothing could break through them. Now that barrier doesn't exist if players are checking their social media at home, and I can see why many of them wouldn't bother being on it at all.

But you have to realise that people who are abusing you are doing it to get their kicks out of it. It's a waste of time listening to them, trying to reason with them or letting it affect you. Abuse says everything about the person abusing and nothing about the person being abused. Why are they abusing you? Because they've got no real power over you, they use their only outlet to try to gain that power. That's either because they want you to fail, or, when it comes to football, maybe because they support a rival club.

You're also someone in the public eye. By the very nature of that, not everyone is going to like you. That's just how it goes, just like you're not going to like everyone else. Some people act like idiots and some people don't, some people express their frustrations in the right way and some don't, wherever you go.

I don't play now, obviously, but I do think that there's been a rise in fan anger. Even when we played at Anfield and they spent the full ninety minutes abusing me, they always clapped me at the start of the match and quite often at the end too. I don't know if that happens as much anymore. But perhaps that's just reflective of the state of the country as a whole.

That said, some of the abuse thrown at footballers – then and now – is unacceptable, and it blows my mind that it's allowed to carry on. Players have grown accustomed to being abused on a very visceral level. Watch any corner being taken by an away player and you'll see it. And some of that abuse goes way too far. I had everything shouted at me – and had most things thrown at me too.

Now there's a certain amount of leeway given, but we've gone well over the limit. It never really affected me, because I was able to use it as motivation to make opposing fans unhappy by us winning the game, but not every player can do that. And, to be honest, they shouldn't have to. It can ruin their confidence and ruin their lives. How is that fair game?

I wouldn't dream of going up to a guy delivering a washing machine to my house and slaughtering him: 'Oh, you're shit, mate, you useless twat. You shouldn't even have this job.' The very idea of anyone doing that is laughable. So why is it acceptable when you go and watch sport and do it? If I walked into my school and told a teacher they were shit and that I hated them, I'd be sacked on the spot. So why have we created a culture of hate in football? We need to make a stand somewhere.

For some reason, we've long allowed footballers to be treated like robots who are somehow immune – or expected to be immune – to the rigours of everyday life and never let it affect their performances on the pitch. But that treatment makes it acceptable for them to accept horrific abuse and be expected to deal with it, no matter what they might be going through in their personal or professional lives. I think about a game I played at Norwich shortly after my mum died and before we'd buried her – I didn't tell the club because I thought that they'd stop me from playing. Nobody in the ground knew what I'd gone through in the previous week. It made me realise that other players must be going through the same things.

Once a player stepped over the white line onto the pitch on matchday, there was always a wilful blindness towards what they were going through away from the game, and I think that's one way in which football hasn't improved. What happens if a player's kid is ill? What happens if the player's experiencing marital problems? What if they're worried that the pressure is starting to get to them? There are so many scenarios that a player might not share with anyone, for whatever reason, and that must be incredibly testing for their mental health.

Nobody ever considers the fact that footballers might suffer from domestic abuse. But why wouldn't that happen? They're often kids who only know how to play football and have less life experience than others. Surely that would make them more vulnerable to mental abuse at home rather than less?

This sort of thing doesn't happen in most other industries. If you're suffering in an office job then you can ask for a little time off; when you come back in, people will know your situation and give you some leeway accordingly. But as a footballer, because of the fact that you're performing in a very public arena, that seems to happen less. When you return, whenever you pull on the shirt, some supporters expect a high level of performance immediately – as soon you go onto the pitch you're expected to be perfect, and if you're not you should expect to be told. That's why you have to learn to put things to one side. Whatever has happened off the pitch has to stay there, because you can't allow the boundaries between different areas of your life to become blurred. If you do, you've got no chance of playing at your best – even the smallest lapses in concentration can make a huge difference on the pitch. But it's really fucking hard to separate things out like that.

You might have lost someone in your family, but nobody thinks about that. It's just, 'He's shit. Why is he playing so shit today?' But if you told the supporters or made some announcement, that might not help either. A club isn't going to say, 'He's going through a divorce, so take that into consideration during the match today.' That's just not how it works.

We played Nottingham Forest at home one year, and the club received a phone call an hour before the match was due to start. Howard Kendall came to see me to tell me that my dad had suffered a huge heart attack and was in hospital. He asked me what I wanted to do – whether I wanted to play or go to the hospital and see him. It was right before the game, and I said that I wanted to play.

By the time I got to the hospital after the match, my dad had passed away and I hadn't been able to see him before he died. I'd missed him. I felt shit.

Howard told me at 2pm, which put me in an awful position because I wanted to do both. But then I also knew that my dad would have wanted me to play in the match, because he'd have done exactly the same. That's just how our family were made. I also knew that I would get judged either way, and I'd judge myself either way too. But nobody in the ground that day knew what I was going through.

You show me a footballer that hasn't had a bad time in life, but you don't even find out about most of them. If someone plays badly or has a poor run of form, it's only ever interpreted as a flaw on their part, and that makes them a target for criticism. We never stop to ask why, and that's incredibly unfair.

Everyone has problems. That's just a part of everyone's lives. And when problems show up, being a footballer doesn't help. Every family is going to have one or more crises that cause heartache and upheaval. Of course the children of high-profile players can get seriously ill, or their partners or parents pass away. We're not immune to the rigours of life.

You look at journalists and supporters and think, 'Maybe if you knew what was going on, you'd take a little more care.' But the players don't want it to be known, because then their private life becomes a media story. They just want to be judged on what they do on the pitch, and keep other areas of their life to themselves. Some people can cope, some people can't. Some want to play, some don't. Everyone is different.

When you stop and think about it, there's an awful lot that goes on behind the other side of the wall. Having played the game, I saw it. But maybe fans and pundits and journalists should take it into consideration too. If they don't know, they don't know. But it's always worth wondering whether there's another reason for what's happening.

Abuse

by Anne-Marie Silbiger

Throw salt at these gaping wounds
I am willing
To take the bait
For a bite of success

5
FAILURE

*'When we can truly embrace failure, learn from
it and move forward to our next goal, we
know we are on the road to success.'*
Sean Molino BCA
(@ForcesFitness)

Failure is something that every footballer has to learn to go through. Early on in your career, it probably makes you try too hard – and hard work remained my default approach right until the end of my career – but at times that hard-work mantra can become suffocating. You end up trying to run through the wall instead of taking a step back and realising that you can just walk around it.

The first thing to do is to stop and say, 'This is shit, and I don't want it to be shit anymore,' and then go back to focusing on enjoying yourself. You'll be amazed what a difference enjoying yourself can make to your form and results – enjoyment and performance levels go hand in hand. Your enjoyment might be linked to the manager, the coaches or whatever else is going on in your life, but you owe it to yourself to control the controllables – you've got to try to make sure you've put yourself in the best possible position to succeed.

For me, positive thinking was always the only answer. It was the only thing that I knew. I've had ten bad games, but the next one will be good. I know you can get to a stage where repeated failure convinces you that you can't do something, but at that point you have to find someone who is able to change your mindset and convince you all over again. They become a key to your improvement, but even then you have to want to change and want to be convinced.

I saw failure as nothing but a bad habit that needed to be addressed, but it's far easier said than done. How do you break that pattern – by hard work, by having fun, or just waiting for your luck to change? There's no right or wrong answer, and you probably need a little of all three. It can be a trial and error process that will turn up some wrong answers. But given that what you were previously doing wasn't working anyway, you might as well go through the process because it's also the only way of finding the right answer.

Some managers are better at identifying the answers quicker than others, with fewer wrong answers, while some have hardwired responses that can do more damage than good. I remember Everton lost 3–0 away in 1994 and I played pretty well, but we were still comfortably beaten. Mike Walker came into the dressing room and told us that we all had to be in the next day, and that we were going to run and run. Is that the right answer, to punish us with physical exertion because we played badly? What about telling us where we went wrong, helping us to understand it and thereby improve our game?

In one of my first games at Torquay in 1998, we got beaten at home and it was utter shit. Wes Saunders was the manager, and again he told us to come in the next day. He ran the legs off the squad, and two of the younger players sustained hamstring injuries. What was proved by doing that, other than that the squad was likely to have fewer options and be more tired for the next game?

In my playing days, running the bollocks off the players was seen by plenty of managers as the only answer. But I worked out that those managers who shouted the loudest were usually the ones trying to hide the fact that they had no knowledge – or perhaps were scared of failure themselves. They weren't getting the players to run and run because it was the *right* answer but because it was their *only* answer, and this passed on the message – which could certainly be demotivating – that the blame always lay with the players.

I remember speaking to a player who came to our club from Darlington, and he said that they used to spend four days during training in midweek wearing sandbags on their backs and barely touching the ball. The theory was that they'd be more hungry for the ball come Saturday, and would feel much lighter on the pitch without the weight on their backs. But that just doesn't work. The added freedom might last for fifteen minutes, but it means that you're not practising the technical side of the game and your bodies are knackered by the extra strain that's put on it midweek.

Instead, a manager has to look outside the box – or maybe within themselves – to try to arrest failure. That might mean anything from tackling the obvious things – changing the system, changing the team, resting certain players, altering the training, examining the matchday preparation – to the minute details – the colour of the dressing rooms, the sleep patterns of the squad, the amount of sunlight they get in their house, the number of video games they're playing. You can take it as far as you like, but it all comes down to the importance of building confidence to eradicate failure. Thankfully, the idea that punishing the players is the best approach seems outdated now.

There's also a need to accept that failure is an inevitable part of sport, and must be treated as such. There's so much that you can control, but there are uncontrollables too. Sometimes a player makes a mistake, sometimes a refereeing decision goes against you, sometimes the opposition are just a bit better. You have to learn to be philosophical about failure and not beat yourself up about it, and you've got to know that you're going to fuck up at some point.

That doesn't mean that it doesn't hurt when it happens, or that you aren't disappointed and don't require a brief period of mourning. Yet when you analyse what went wrong, you might have to conclude that you played really well ... but your opponents were simply better than you. Is that really failure, or is it only failure if you didn't do the best you could?

The best thing a goalkeeper can do is accept that failure is guaranteed. That sounds defeatist, but it's actually the opposite. You know you'll make mistakes, so you must be ready for them. Goalkeepers should be their own greatest critics. They know their games inside out and are therefore aware if they've made a mistake, even if it doesn't lead to a goal or a chance. If you're not honest with yourself, you'll get found out because you'll keep making the same mistakes – and eventually they'll cost your team.

One of the biggest questions regarding failure is whether you let it cling to you throughout your career. So rather than shedding it as you go, you let it – or part of it – pile up on your shoulders and it never leaves you. Take someone like Theo Walcott, who was a golden boy at eighteen and wanted to be the main man for England. Do players like him still think about being eighteen again and having all their careers in front of them? Or do they reason that what is done is done, be proud of everything they've achieved and continue with their commitment to being the best they can be? Because if it's the former, that's going to make things harder for them.

I felt different as a player at Everton to how I did at Torquay years later. At Torquay I realised that dropping down the leagues was part of ageing; I felt like a father figure and so I learnt new ways to enjoy the experience. But some footballers might see playing at a club in a lower division as a failure and struggle to cope with it. It has the potential to play on their minds and any setbacks can easily take over a player's psyche.

If I was going through a bad time on the pitch, I'd just take myself away, sit somewhere quietly and think, 'Right, I'm obviously struggling here, so how do I go about changing it?' If I started panicking, it was more likely to get worse than better. I'd start coming for balls that I shouldn't through a desire to make a positive impact, or try to do extra things that wouldn't actually help me. I reasoned that if I just tried to relax and enjoy it, then I'd be all the better for it – or what's the point in playing at all? During those times you think about why it all matters so much to you, and what and who you do it for.

The only way to improve as a goalkeeper, as a player or as a person is to self-analyse, but to do so in a positive way that leaves you prepared to move forward. That's one of the hardest things, because it involves facing up to a reality that can be unpleasant. But hiding away from it is the one surefire way to miss out on the chance to improve.

So you resolve to go out and have fun, and certainly not try anything new. Slowly but surely, you can come back round and dial the pressure down on yourself, and it gets better. But it's extremely difficult not to try too hard, especially when you're younger. You occasionally get left out of the team, and the first time it happens it makes you push too hard and question yourself. The second time, you think, 'OK, what's happening here? How did I deal with this last time?'

In November 1982 we played Liverpool at Goodison. We'd actually started the season pretty well at home, although we had dropped silly points to Brighton and drawn to Newport County in the League Cup. Our away form was poor, losing five of our first six away from Goodison. But everyone felt good going into the derby.

It was a disaster. It still remains the worst match in living memory for plenty of Evertonians. We lost 5–0, had Glenn Keeley sent off after half an hour and Ian Rush scored four goals against me. The whole game was a nightmare for the team, and understandably the supporters let us know how angry they were.

I actually didn't think I played too badly, and I can't recall making any bad mistakes during the game. I didn't watch it back because I couldn't face watching the humiliation, but I always knew if I'd made a mistake and I don't remember anything else I could really have done about the goals. I'd gone into the match suffering from a toe injury. I'd been getting ulcerated toes for a while after joining Everton, sometimes right down to the bone. My feet would swell up during matches and then afterwards they'd turn a horrible colour and I'd be in agony. I'd wear flip-flops rather than shoes to let them air and heal, but I went into that Liverpool game in particular pain. I ended up going to hospital after the match, where they carried out a medical procedure that involved them forcibly pulling my toes apart.

Howard Kendall responded by dropping me from the first team. He didn't really speak much to me about it, but then that's just the way he was. He believed that my form had dipped enough to give Jim Arnold a go in goal, and there wasn't much I could do other than accept it and work harder to get my place back. I was never one to go ranting and raving to the manager and demand my place back.

But the worst thing about being dropped was that it just meant that I had so much time on my hands. I wasn't interested in golf or anything like that that the other lads did. I'd just go home, watch TV, read a book, drink tea and walk the dogs. But you're always thinking about not being in the team. Everything that goes through your mind during those other activities is about wanting to play on a Saturday and not being able to.

I didn't ever worry about my long-term future at the club because I knew that I was good enough – and the decision was out of my hands anyway. I couldn't affect it. I just had to refuse to accept my fate, double down on the work and prove the manager wrong by becoming a better player. I went on loan to Port Vale, which gave me some competitive minutes.

Eventually, Jim picked up an injury with four games of the season remaining, and I came back into the team. We won three of our remaining four games, I played well and kept my place. It took Jim's misfortune for me to get a go, but it was all down to my continued focus that it worked out well for me. If I'd taken my eye off the ball or allowed my level of professionalism to drop, I wouldn't have been able to take that chance as I did. I had played the leading role in reversing my failure.

That Liverpool game also taught me to use failure as a motivational tool to keep myself sharp. Whenever we subsequently played against Liverpool, the 5–0 loss was always in the front of my mind. For some players, this might be a bad thing. They might let the failure haunt them and make them freeze in fear of making another mistake that costs the team in such a big game. But I was the opposite. I'd be thinking, 'That match fucked up my career for a while and put everything I'd worked towards at risk. I'm not letting you do that again.' It became a matter of revenge for me, punishing Liverpool for what they'd done.

Throughout my career I tried to break down each season into three-game blocks where I didn't make a mistake. That enabled me to maintain total focus across those three matches, and then I'd start again. And I reasoned that if I made three mistakes or fewer in a season, I could probably make up for those goals or points with saves that people didn't expect me to make. So each season, if I kept that up, I'd always finish level or slightly above.

Those principles also have to apply to the team as a whole. People in football often bemoan the fact that they're on a losing streak. But again, it's about processing past experience to shape the future. OK, you're on a losing streak, but that means that the end's in sight. We're not getting further away from a win, we're getting nearer to one. You've lost six matches on the bounce? Well, then you're due one, aren't you?

It's how you look at things, and in football you have to be positive or you're already inviting failure. If you've lost the last six matches – or lost 5–0 to Liverpool – you can't go out onto the pitch believing that you're going to struggle again, although many do. You think, 'Brilliant, this is an immediate chance to put things right.' Now that's hard, mentally, particularly if something goes wrong in the first five minutes. But that's where your belief comes in, and all your physical and mental preparation becomes incredibly valuable.

It's also when the environment in which you're working becomes important. Going back to Mike Walker's Everton team in 1994, we played a certain way; it wasn't that we were a bad team, but the system was hopeless. We'd play ten, twenty, thirty passes in our own half, but eventually one would go astray or we'd be broken down and the opposition would score. That was poor judgement on his part initially, but it was also a mistake not to look at what we had and work on a solution after the system had been shown to fail. Use the team as an experiment.

Fortunately, Joe Royle came in and changed the system completely. He looked to get the ball quickly and told us to press the ball more proactively. Everything was positive. We were constantly pushing forward, constantly playing fast football, and we learnt to believe that our opponents couldn't cope with that. Everything was positive; negative thoughts were expelled. We won the FA Cup, conceding one goal in the entire competition, and we were never behind. Never for a minute in that run did we believe that we wouldn't win the cup.

You can see the differences in these approaches all around us, right up to the top of society. I occasionally look on Twitter and see some individuals who have gone way above and beyond for other people, and I've come into contact with others who have done the bare minimum and then moved on. If someone is suffering, is in need of help and feels that they aren't being given sufficient support from others, it can exacerbate any mental anguish they might have. And that can have a devastating impact on their life.

Although I felt that I'd put myself in the right place mentally to deal with failure, it's clear that every player and person is different. That presents unique challenges. Sport is unlike most professions, because of the extreme highs and lows it creates and the very public character of those extremes. I might go into work now and have a good day or a bad day, I might even have a really shitty day, but the extremes are much less dramatic than within sport. In football, you can go from euphoria to abject failure in a matter of days – or even over the course of one game. And that can be hard for some players to cope with.

If the FA, Premier League and English Football League have – or need to have – procedures in place on racism, homophobia and mental health, then they also need to be an international rescue service on a number of other topics, and that includes the subject of failure. We talk about proaction, and that's certainly necessary, but they also need to be a reactive rescue service when players, managers and clubs require them. These organisations have the ability to sit outside the club structure and parachute people in to look after individuals. That's how you demonstrate true leadership.

And that must extend to all players, right through the club structure. The clubs have their own agendas, and always will. If you have a player at sixteen who has all the talent in the world, they're more likely to be looked after brilliantly. If you're an average player, you'll get binned. Such treatment isn't based on equality, it's based on talent, and this creates a vicious cycle. It's increasingly difficult for players not to become mercenary when the clubs are mercenary themselves. Loyalty is a two-way street after all, and it has been eroded from both ends. The game at academy level is a cattle market, and when you're past your sell-by date and of no further use, you're out the door. For some players, coping with that failure is incredibly difficult.

It becomes harder still when so much of it is based on sheer luck. Let's say two scouts go to a match. One might really rate a full-back and the other might not rate him quite as highly. The future of the player depends on the scout that rates him most highly working for a club that has the funds to sign him and for which full-back is a problem position. The player can't control that, but the mechanics of that one scouting mission might define his professional life. How do you deal with that? How do you process it? If you're not signed by a club, you can tell yourself that it's only one person's opinion, that it doesn't make you any worse as a player. But that's a very hard thing to do, especially when you're young. That kind of thing can affect a kid very deeply.

There has to be a watertight system for helping all of these kids: those who don't make the grade at academy level, those who fall away from the first-team picture and drop down the leagues, those who sustain serious injuries that hamper their careers and force them into extended periods of intense rehabilitation. Expert counselling is needed at each stage.

And then there are the people giving the bad news. How must it feel to repeatedly tell young people that the thing they've dreamed about doing is no longer going to be possible, to be the bearer of such devastating news? Those people need counsellors on hand too. A failure to put that framework in place risks creating a mental health crisis in football. And unlike other industries, the financial resources are there to create a support network for all. Clubs owe their employees and stakeholders that support network.

Failure

by Anne-Marie Silbiger

In hours of
enduring failure
Extricate what you can from the spoils of
  labour
Sporting triumph in quiet glory later

6

IMPROVEMENT

'Even at the top of our game we can always
self-improve, work hard, set goals and
maintain our vision.'
Sean Molino BCA
(@ForcesFitness)

If a group of kids came up to you, what would you look for in order to build a rapport with them? It depends what they're wearing, what they show you of their personalities. One of them might have a pair of Nike trainers on, so I'd tell them I had a pair of trainers like that. One of them has a Manchester United shirt, and I tell them I could never have supported Manchester United because I played for Everton or that I was lucky enough to have played with Ryan Giggs in the Wales national team.

But it goes beyond that. Look at how they walk, how they carry themselves, who is near the front and who is near the back, which one is the loudest and which is keeping quiet and virtually hidden towards the back of the group.

As soon as you meet them you're picking up on clues that then enable you to work out the dynamics of the group as a whole, and that's vital for establishing a rapport with them.

As soon as I meet someone, my brain is whirring to take in information. Everyone does that. Everyone sees things, but maybe everybody doesn't take it all in.

If I've got a group of new kids that I'm going to coach, one of the first things I look for in them is the noise level within the group and in the individuals. If they're all excited, that's great; I can probably do what I want in terms of coaching because they'll be open to suggestion. But if some are a bit quiet, or they don't have the right gear on, you can work with that too. You engage with them differently, set them different targets. Kids can be cruel. So you take one of the ones that looks to be in charge of the group, and you bring them aside and tell them that you want them to help a quieter kid. And you say to the stronger one, 'That kid might not be the best, but I know your quality and I think you can help them out and help them improve. I want you to be their teacher.' If you're pairing them up for a particular drill, then you might pair up the quieter and the noisier one.

When I was coaching the goalkeepers at Margate, I had one group of kids who were aged up to around twelve, and then everyone else. I immediately realised that I didn't want that, and merged the two groups. I probably wasn't meant to combine them, but it worked out well. What will that teach the older ones? Patience, and the ability to reflect on how far they've come as they're trying to teach a younger lad. It teaches them to work out the problems of another person, which in turn makes them more likely to analyse their own flaws. The younger kids will want to work at the pace of the older ones, so they'll strive to work at a higher tempo. It will also get them used to playing against bigger children; this can be vital for a young goalkeeper, who will have to get used to jumping between bodies and diving at the feet of strikers. Of course, you still have to manage the individuals, particularly the younger ones. They have to know that you're there to talk through their problems, and you need to stay vigilant to identify those who might be struggling in this environment. But suddenly I had ten coaches rather than one. We weren't playing matches as a mixed group, where it would have become too competitive, but it made the older goalkeepers think about giving something back to the younger kids. I'm sure they'd have appreciated this at the same age.

But it does more than that. As a goalkeeper, you have to establish effective communication skills because you're playing behind four or five defenders who need a positive relationship with you. That defence might comprise of a bunch of completely different characters, and you have to learn how to deal with each of them individually. There's probably one that you can bollock when they make a mistake and be sure they will react positively, another you have to put an arm around and build up.

If you ask a goalkeeper at sixteen what their team is like, they should know. How does the centre-forward like to have the ball kicked to him? What's the personality of your two full-backs? Which midfielder is the best in the air? Which centre-back can you shout at and rely on them getting the message to their defensive colleagues? They should know all of this because they ought to have built up the relationships that help them to learn it all.

The same skill also enables you to do the same with regard to the opposition. In the first five minutes, a player is sizing up their opponents, and the faster he does this the better. Is he quicker than me, is he stronger than me, how should I play to counteract it if he's either – or both – of these things, or, if I'm the quicker and stronger one, how do I maximise this to my team's advantage? Should I be pressing him or sitting off? Should I tackle harder or softer? Should I go for aerial duels with him or not? The best players do all of this almost instantly. At the professional level in the modern game, scouting reports and your own experience will already have taught you much of what you need to know. But kids should be taught how to do this as they learn the game, and that 'Margate strategy' works with this too. By coaching other goalkeepers, they learn to identify characteristics in other players' games rather than purely focusing on their own.

I was very fortunate with the coaches that I got to work with: Gordon Banks, Peter Bonetti, Jim Barron, Alan Kelly and Alan Hodgkinson – they all brought different things to the table. They were all good goalkeeping coaches, but of course some suited me better than others – that's the nature of things.

I worked with Bob Wilson at Wales, and sometimes if a coach was too nice, as with Bob, I didn't like it. That was no fault on his part. He was a lovely guy, but I'd sometimes worry that he was so friendly that he might avoid criticising me or finding fault with my game. A large part of a coach's job is to identify flaws and motivate players to work on them. That will inevitably cause the odd clash and disagreement. I also worked with Mark Wallington for a while, who had been at Leicester City and competed with Peter Shilton for a first-team place. He would tell me that 'Shilton did this' and 'Shilton did that', or that 'Shilton would never let a shot in in training'. But I didn't care. I only cared about performing between 3pm and 5pm on a Saturday, and telling me about another goalkeeper was never going to have any impact on me. Those coaches would quickly learn that I had a certain way of doing things that worked well for me and worked well for Everton.

Howard Kendall was always good with me, because there was perfect honesty between us. He might come in at half-time or full-time and say, 'How the fuck did you let that goal go in?' but then we would both go away and watch the game back. By Monday morning, he might come and tell me that he'd watched it again and that he was wrong, or I might go to him and say exactly the same. The give and take of respect there was really healthy. Howard knew that one thing that made me angry was bullshit, because bullshitting someone never got anyone to perform at their best.

But I've found that the key to improvement is creating an environment where it isn't only coach-based learning. You have the first-team goalkeeper, the lad sat on the bench, one or two beneath them and then the apprentices, and if you're clever you can learn off all of them every day. They might say something that you haven't thought of.

I used to do some ridiculous tackles in training, nowhere near the man but just outlandish high dives across the air. I did the same when training with Wales too, but it had a purpose there. I remember playing against Crystal Palace, who had my Wales compatriot Chris Coleman playing for them. Maybe Chris remembered me from training, because one time I ran screaming out for a cross and he ducked so I could get the ball. Maybe it was nothing to do with Wales training, but maybe it was *everything* to do with it. I was always trying to find a way to get an edge, and as a goalkeeper it helps to be intimidating.

When I played, I'd know the opponents instantly. Take Wimbledon, for example. If I was playing them, I knew that they were going to get the ball into the box as many times as they could. Was I going to catch everything with so many bodies in the box? Probably not. So I'd already prepared the central defenders, telling them that they should stay nearer to me than they normally would. That way, if the ball did come loose in the box because a striker challenged me, we'd have a better chance of getting it clear without conceding a chance.

On a good day, my plans would work out perfectly and we all went home happy, while the defenders had greater confidence in me because they recognised that I foresaw any potential problems and produced proactive solutions rather than merely reacting in real time. Let's take another example: say I knew I was going to face an opponent whose manager liked to utilise long throw-ins. Where should I stand? If I'd studied him and knew who he liked to throw it to, I'd go and stand next to that person, put my hands in the air and make it clear to the thrower that I was aware of his plan. The thrower then had to make a decision – maybe he'd throw it shorter or flatter than he was intending to. Even just by standing somewhere different I could give him a problem. And as soon as he went back to throw it, I'd have moved back to where I was intending to be anyway. It all comes down to passing on the problem to the opposition.

I ask my goalkeepers what their first thought is when the opening corner of the match is about to be delivered. It shouldn't be where the defenders are standing or who they're marking, because that should already have been organised beforehand. It should be identifying the signal of the corner-taker. If he puts one arm up and crosses the ball to the back post, I know that the next time he puts one arm up I should prepare to move to the back post, perhaps even shout that I'm prepared for a back-post corner. You might change their mind, you might not. But you do give them something new to think about with just a little forethought.

I also talk to them about one-on-ones, and ask if they ever dummy the forwards. Most people, maybe even some goal-keepers, assume that it will always be the striker dummying the goalkeeper, but it can work the other way round. If you lean slightly to one side, the forward might think he has a better chance of shooting the other way or try to round you that way. It's only a slight trigger movement that you imme-diately rectify, but you put a doubt in the striker's mind.

In short, you have to treat every match like a game of chess. Read it in exactly the same way. As soon as their full-back gets the ball, it's his move. You've got to work out what he's most likely to want to do, what his alternative options are and what *you* want him to do. At that point we can move players around to affect the full-back's decision, to proac-tively shape his next move.

Here's an example: as soon as a penalty was given away by my team, I'd immediately kick the ball down the field or into the crowd while the referee was still managing the penalty decision. If I needed to claim that I hadn't heard the whistle,

I could easily do that. If there was a little scuffle or some debate between the players and the referee about the award of the penalty, I'd walk as far away from the goal as I could before being called back, and then I'd walk slowly back to the goal. Without touching or interacting with the penalty taker, I was taking a small amount of control away from him. That loss of control creates doubt.

I remember speaking to Andy Hinchcliffe at Everton and asking him whether in the warm-up at an away ground he counted the steps he'd be able to take to deliver a corner. I told him that if I was a corner-taker, whenever I played away at a new ground I would go to every corner of the pitch and work out how close the corner flag was to the stands and make a note of it in a little book. Every ground is different, after all. Then the next time I was playing there, I'd know how many steps I'd be able to take to deliver a corner. And all week in the build-up to the game, when I practised my corners, I'd limit myself to that number of steps.

The first thing I did in the morning, if we were playing at home, was to look out the window for a minute. What was the weather like? Was the ball more likely to skip on or hold up. Did I need to be careful of backpasses stopping short? Was the sun likely to be in my eyes. When I look at goalkeepers now, I wonder if those thought processes are still there. In fact, the first thing I did when I got to the ground was to check which way the flags were blowing. I'd throw and kick the ball around, and work out where the wind was taking it. I knew then that in one half I might be able to catch the ball quickly and throw it almost past the half-way line and start a counter-attack, while in the other half I might have to play it short to feet.

I remember a game I played at Highbury against Arsenal in 1992/93. We lost 2–0, and Ian Wright scored early on to give Arsenal the lead. But later in the same game, Wright cut inside and fired a shot at goal. That day, I'd looked at the weather forecast and saw that the pitch would probably be heavy and that it would rain before the game, so the ball was almost certainly going to be slippy. On a bright sunny day, I'd have tried to catch Wright's shot. But because of the weather I knew that, even though I would most likely have caught the ball, there was a chance of it slipping through my hands. I also knew that if I caught it and slid along the heavy pitch, the ball might slip free – and Wright was lightning quick to pick up on things like that. So through my preparation, I'd already decided that any shots like that from him would be punched away from goal.

I was also probably wearing different boots. When I was at Everton I used to wear leather boots. They weighed a lot, and we were often playing on pitches that were heavy. So I asked the boot suppliers to give me some pairs of the cheapest boots they had, which were a plastic type. I'd use the plastic boots on those days, because they were waterproof and had no weight to them, so my feet wouldn't be lumbered down by sodden, heavy boots. That might allow me to jump an extra inch higher, the difference between claiming a cross or not. They didn't last long, but that didn't matter to me. On a pleasant day, or on a less heavy pitch, the leather ones would work better and probably ensure that my kicking was more accurate.

* * *

Goalkeepers should be the biggest thinkers in the game. They can see the whole pitch in front of them, but they also have the greatest control of any player over their performance. The success of a striker might depend on how he's playing, but also on the ability of the midfielders to keep the ball, the wingers to beat their man and cross it accurately, the defence to win back possession. For a goalkeeper, it's more about you versus them. It's also the most scrutinised position on the pitch, where every mistake can be disastrous and the margin for error is non-existent. You're placed in no-win situations, where a save is mere expectation and a non-save a bad error. A striker can miss an easy chance, score the next one and still be the hero, but if a goalkeeper misses an easy save it defines his match. That means you have to think about everything to give yourself the best chance of succeeding.

I hate goalkeepers that don't think. Of course, sometimes you have to play on instinct, because one of your teammates might make a mistake that you cannot plan for. But you can prepare for most things. That's why I quite like young players who I've coached that are prepared to push the boundaries of the rules, because it shows that they're thinking about everything. It's about controlling the controllables. If you've ensured that you cannot be surprised by anything that an opponent tries, have done everything within your control to impact upon their behaviour and have prepared yourself perfectly for the match, you can be sure that you've given it your best. Nobody can ask any more than that, and you cannot ask more than that of yourself.

It all comes down to knowing people and communicating with people; with yourself, your teammates and your opponents. And it's the same – or at least similar – whether it's a Wimbledon player trying to score via a long throw-in or trying to help someone suffering from anxiety and attempting to get them out of bed.

Here's an example about knowing how to communicate and tailoring your behaviour to the individual. I went on a suicide awareness course once, and it was great. We were all told to close our eyes, and they asked one person what his approach would be if he encountered someone standing on the side of a bridge. He had lots of good answers, to be fair to him. They then asked us to open our eyes and imagine that the person standing in front of us was on a ledge, as if they were about to jump. They asked the same guy to come forward and go through everything he'd said when he had his eyes closed in practice. It was much harder for him because it was more like a real-life scenario.

They asked me to do it, and I said that I'd tell little lies if I had to. I'd check out the person's shoes, their jewellery, their hair, the clothes they were wearing. And then if they didn't respond to my initial questions about coming down or coming closer to me, I'd use that information and weave it into little conversations. I'd say, 'My missus has got a pair of trainers like that,' or I'd ask, 'Your hair – do you ever wear it curly or do you always straighten it?' Because I think sometimes you're more likely to get answers to questions like that, and it can begin a dialogue in a natural, unforced way.

But that's just my way of doing things, picking up on little details and focusing on them. And that goes back to coaching kids at football, doing exactly the same thing. It's all about making connections with people. Some people think that sport is just sport, but that just isn't true. Sport is life.

You also have to be prepared to think outside the box, and be rewarded for doing so. In order to try to gain an advantage, I looked into how other sportspeople trained. Boxing was one of the main sports I researched. Obviously, the violence and punching elements weren't relevant, but plenty was: controlled aggression, the movement, how boxers prepare mentally to hurt someone, and how they get hurt. I also looked into weightlifting, for the strength and conditioning training, and gymnastics for the power that gymnasts have while being incredibly light on their feet. Golf was all about concentration. I was asked to concentrate for ninety minutes on a Saturday, but in fact it was about having total concentration for a few moments at a time and just being alert the rest of the time. Golfers might have a five-hour round where they do nothing for five minutes, then they have a few moments that can define their round and maybe their entire week.

Golf was also interesting because it taught me to think of my foot as the head of a golf club. With my distribution, I learnt to use different parts of my foot in different ways to play passes a certain way. That might sound obvious now, but practising chips and drives with my feet really helped my game. I thought of teammates as golf holes, where I'd need to land the ball at a certain speed and angle to arrive at their feet or chests perfectly.

The older you get, the more you should look at external things to try to gain an advantage, and the further outside the box you might have to look. But these are the things that you can pass on to young goalkeepers who might not have thought to do that.

Howard Kendall once said to me that I needed to 'stop trying to be perfect' and be happy with the level I was at. I didn't agree with him then, and I still don't now, because I would never stop trying to improve. I think what he meant was that he wanted me to chill out a bit and not do everything with such intensity; that I should be pleased with how I was playing rather than always looking to do more.

But I was a perfectionist. As soon as the season ended, I was pissed off. Some players might like to go off on an end-of-season tour and get pissed, before lazing around for a few weeks. I was the complete opposite. I'd seen them all have a few beers on the coach enough times during the season, so I didn't need to go abroad to watch them do it again every day but somewhere hotter. Football was everything I wanted, and for two months it was taken away from me. All I craved was to be back playing. I wasn't interested in anything else. I know some players needed to recharge and players now demand rest, but that was never for me. I would vote for football being played on every weekend of the year. I couldn't see the point in me having a break when I wasn't tired – and football was what I was good at.

But one of the difficulties of training in sport is that there's no such thing as perfection. You can't get to 100 per cent, and you can never complete your training or say that your performances on matchday were perfect. There's always another level that you can take yourself to, always another trophy to win or a new season to start. It never stops, and psychologically that can be a draining thing to manage.

But that's just me. I hate it when people say that they can't do things before they've even tried. If you think that, you'll never do it, and you're only making it harder anyway. As soon as you put barriers in the way of people, or they erect them themselves, they shut down. As a goalkeeper, you have to believe that you can make the impossible saves possible. As long as you work hard at it, why can't you do anything?

Mental health is an area in which you have to keep telling people that you believe in them, that you're with them and that they can do things, not that they can't. That's the only way, because when people feel anxious or depressed they cling to negativity more than positivity.

People generally look for reasons why things can't happen and why they can't do this or that, and society is structured to make some people believe that this negative way of thinking is correct. I have Everton fans who come up to me and ask whether we can win on Saturday, and my answer is always the same: 'Well, why not?' Give me a reason why we can't and I'll give you a reason why we can.

Because if you don't think that you can do something, psychologically you're already set up to fail. And when you repeatedly start anything with that mindset, it warps into, 'Well, why should I bother trying?' I'd much rather people begin challenges believing that they can succeed, but that often requires them to be helped.

If you help someone to go into anything with a positive mental attitude, you vastly increase their chances of succeeding – and might also teach them that next time they can believe in their success without as much help. And if you give something your very best, there's nothing further that you can do.

Improvement

by Anne-Marie Silbiger

Keep your head down
Let chaos reign elsewhere
Work on your goals
Stay quiet of your dreams

7

MOTIVATION

*'Some days it will feel emotionally and physically
exhausting, but on those days keep going, keep
talking and know that feeling will pass.'*
Hope Virgo, author and mental health campaigner
(@HopeVirgo)

There's no such thing as the finished article. Every player,
from amateur to international level, can always improve.
Unfortunately, some people tend to settle for far less than
their best. They make the grade in whatever line of work
they're in, and then they tend to coast. They sit back and
congratulate themselves on making it. But many of the best
players in the game's history have been hardworking to the
point of obsession.

My attitude has always been this: If you're not very good
at something, strive to be better. If you are good at something,
strive to be even better. If you're very good at something,
strive to be the best. Surely it makes sense to go on that journey, because the journey itself is rewarding and so is the destination. If that means staying an extra hour at work, so be it.
If you have the time, why wouldn't that help? If you stay
longer and other people doing the same job don't, it might

make you better than them at it. Having time is great, but what's the point if you don't use it? Otherwise it's just a waste.

So I've always warmed towards players who were not necessarily the most talented but had an incredible work ethic and will to win. Of everyone I played with, Barry Horne stands out for Everton and Wales. Barry was an incredibly clever bloke and the most intense person I've ever met. His brain never stopped whirring. He wasn't exactly a graceful or elegant footballer, but he was incredibly effective. He squeezed absolutely everything out of what he had. He was brave and hard and incredibly committed. We played Swindon, and someone kicked him and their stud went into his calf, leaving a bleeding hole. Barry just got the physio to fill the hole with cotton wool and then he ran back onto the pitch to carry on. If Barry hadn't had that personality, he'd never have played so much for his country and in the Premier League. But he tackled anything that moved, got into the faces of the opposition and would run from minute one to ninety to try to help his team over the line. Every team benefits from that kind of dedication.

And then there's the complete opposite. At Everton we signed a defender in 1997. As soon as he arrived at the club, he made it clear to us that he wasn't bothered about playing. It seemed that he was happy to have signed for a Premier League club, got his big move and decent wages, and had decided he'd done enough.

He was a good player, but for whatever reason he just didn't want it. It started with a few niggling injuries, but it became a bit silly. The gaffer told him that he was going to play for the reserves because he was fit, and then during the training session before the match he said that his back had gone. After one season we sold him on.

I look back now and wonder what was going on there. Was it really the case that he just decided that he wasn't bothered about playing, or was there something else blocking him? Was he scared of playing at the highest level? Was the pressure too much for him in the Premier League? Was it all bravado? Or was he just pretending that he wanted to take the money and relax in order to disguise his lack of confidence? Maybe it was all too much for him, moving to Everton. His old club might have accepted the offer to sell because they needed the money, and the player didn't get much choice. You look back and wonder whether you'd been reading the situation all wrong.

No footballer ever struggles to get motivated for cup finals, season-defining games or derby days. It was never the biggest matches that you had to get motivated for, but the smaller ones. On derby day on Merseyside, I'd drive to Goodison and the whole city was buzzing. Everyone was wearing shirts or carrying their scarves, and you were met with cheers when you arrived at the club. On those days, the dressing room had an atmosphere that told you that every player had no problem whatsoever with motivation.

But at other times you did sense that something extra was needed. When you were playing in front of fewer than 10,000 supporters on a plastic pitch and it was pissing down with rain, that's when you needed to be at your best and when preparation was most important. Because those were the victories that won you titles. Physically, those matches might not have been any harder, but psychologically they were. You and your team might be the opposition's cup final, and allowing complacency or negative thoughts to creep in gave your opponent an advantage that they didn't deserve. Players in the squad might have been a little complacent, and every manager will tell you that complacency kills consistency.

Duncan Ferguson was a great example of this. Duncan was one of the best strikers in the country. If he'd played Manchester United or Liverpool every week, he would have been the best. He scored five times against Liverpool and scored more goals against Manchester United than against any other team. But there was something within him that meant he didn't thrive as much against the smaller clubs, in the games where he should have been scoring most of his goals. It just didn't quite have the same buzz for him to play in those matches. He was like Frank Sinatra: brilliant on a Las Vegas stage, but probably not quite at the same level in Coventry.

To win the league in my day, you had to smash Oldham, Luton Town, Southampton and the like. If you look at the league every season, it's often the dropped points against the teams in the bottom six that stops you winning the title. If I could sense that some of the players might not be at their best because it was *only* Oldham, I'd know that I had to be extra vigilant because someone might make a silly mistake or I might be busier than expected. I could use my teammates as extra motivation.

The hardest matches for me weren't cup finals, derbies or international qualifiers, but friendlies. I hated them, because I always felt that I had more to lose than gain. A good performance wouldn't make much difference, but a bad performance would. Those were the matches when you needed to be motivated the most, yet they were the hardest to get motivated for.

Maintaining motivation isn't just as easy as being on your guard, though. Because you know that it only lasts so far, you have to keep changing your motivation to stay at your hungriest, and that can be very difficult if nobody shows you how to do it. Let's say you have a piece of music that gets you going. How long will it get you going for and, more importantly, how quickly can you tell when it's stopped being 100 per cent effective?

It's also a question of balance. If you wake up in the morning and feel great, that can perversely be really hard to deal with – because how do you sustain feeling great all day? There's only one direction in which to travel from great. So extrapolate from that: if you're feeling great in the warm-up between 2pm and 3pm, you might find it really hard to maintain that feeling until 5pm, when the game finishes. Maybe it's better to be on edge in the warm-up, because by 3pm you can explode and be at 100 per cent. Does it matter if I let in ten goals in the warm-up? No, because no fucker has ever paid me for the warm-up. And nobody has ever paid me for training either. That's all just a prelude to the match, and your performance in the match is what you get paid for.

When I was at Bradford City I used to coach Gary Walsh, and in the warm-up he'd even put me on edge. If you threw him the ball and he dropped it, he'd have to do another ten or fifteen catches before he felt happy again. So in training on Friday, I'd ask him how many catches he needed to be happy. Do you need ten, twenty, forty, sixty, a hundred? Maybe he didn't have an answer. When we started, I told him that whenever he was happy we would stop. He was worried that if we only did ten he wouldn't be ready. But ten good ones and you go away from here in a positive mindset. What's the point in doing more than that, and risk moving away from that happiness and comfort? My job is to get you ready for tomorrow, nothing else. So if you do ten catches and you're happy, go in. If the manager then comes and moans and asks why he's gone in early, I'll tell him. But people don't; they do a hundred of these and a hundred of those, blindly. But in what way does that re-create the environment of a match? And in what way does blindly doing that ensure that they'll be in the right frame of mind if they drop one of the last five?

You get coaches who know what drills they like to coach and how they think these drills work, but they forget that each individual goalkeeper is an individual person who will react to things differently. If drills are all it's about I'll go and get a sheepdog, because they can do them perfectly.

I hear people saying that a goalkeeper they've worked with would never let a goal in during training, but that never impressed me. Maybe it's a good sign, but then maybe it isn't. Maybe he's trying so hard in training that by Saturday he can't maintain it. Maybe if he doesn't let a goal in during training, when he inevitably concedes on a Saturday it will cause an adverse psychological reaction because he hasn't conditioned himself to produce a positive response.

One thing that might motivate players is professional jealousy. I think there's a degree of that within every football club, because we're only human. We all envy things other people have or can do that we struggle to match, and these becomes the carrots that we chase. Football is a team sport, and there's a cliché that every player must be motivated purely by the team's success. But individual motivation within a team environment is perfectly acceptable and can undoubtedly help the team. I was lucky because the players competing for my position at Everton were good people. Jim Arnold, for example, had come from non-league exactly like me, and we had an understanding that whoever got picked, the other would fully support them. That's just the way it was. We knew what it was like to do a 'proper, real-world job', so we considered it important to look after each other.

But then jealousy is one of the reasons for creating a squad of players with effective competition for places. A manager wants individuals to be annoyed that they're not hitting the same levels as their teammates, because it will push them to strive harder in training and get better. If you're a striker and you're not scoring goals but the other striker is, I'm sure there's some jealousy that goes through your mind because you're taught to be hungry to play and hungry to succeed. But I always thought that if Jim played well and was in the team, he should stay there. At the end of the day we're a team, not individuals, and you have to pull in the same direction. It becomes very hard when individual players are very obviously putting themselves before the team, and that isn't acceptable in terms of motivation. The team always has to be the end goal.

I think that individualism is more prevalent now, because players are taught to be more ambitious and demand instant success. Combine that with the increase in player power, and that creates the culture of the individual. There probably were a couple of players that I played with who were focused on their careers away from Everton, but the manager soon got rid of them.

I think if you take it the right way, jealousy can be a really useful tool to put a fire under players and eliminate any complacency. The problems start when that jealousy comes from players who are spoilt and believe that they should command a certain status within a squad without working hard. The best players in the world do all the hard work first before they're good players. At times, some players can forget that.

I don't think it necessarily comes down to a good manager to give players confidence, but good pairings and good groups of people working intelligently together are vital. Howard Kendall had Colin Harvey, Joe Royle had Willie Donachie. Alex Ferguson changed his assistants over the course of his tenure to match the needs of the squad and the changes in the game, as well as to make sure he got the best out of himself. The No. 2 becomes the bridge to the manager, so the manager has to have the right ideas and the assistants have to be able to get that message across in the right way.

But the manager has to be prepared to try new things to maintain belief. When I went into a club, I'd look at the fixture list and work out when we were going to have to train hard and when we wouldn't be able to. In the middle of a tough training run, I'd take the goalkeepers to play badminton or volleyball doubles. It gave their brains a rest from typical training drills. If you do the same thing over and over again, it eventually becomes hard work – and hard work can be unenjoyable.

A goalkeeper needs to be a footballer (distribution), an athlete (sprinting out of goal to clear), a rugby player (catching and throwing) and a volleyball player (punching). Goalkeeping asks more of a player than any other position, and any weakness will be exposed. These goalkeepers used to put more effort into badminton and volleyball than they did into normal training. They were having a laugh and buzzing to try to beat their teammates, but more importantly they weren't thinking about football for a morning. It gave them a mental break while still being a form of training – they were still working on their hand–eye coordination, still working on communication because they were playing doubles, still working on their movement and their jumping and landing. But it's just more fun. How couldn't that help?

If you're lucky enough to have any role within a football club, why wouldn't you make sure that you know absolutely everything you possibly can to make life easier? For example, I believe that there should be a former player, one who's still close to the fanbase, employed to advise the chairperson or owner and let them know where the fans are at. Not just the extreme opinions, but as a gauge of majority opinion. What he tells them doesn't have to define the decisions they make, but it can certainly make them better informed.

The manager should have someone who sits in the crowd, and then goes and sees them before they do their post-match press conferences and tells them what the real reaction of the fans is. Sometimes it's obvious to them anyway, but occasionally it might not be.

If you go out there and claim that the team played well when they didn't, you've got no chance. But if you go out there and are honest, you have. You've got issues if problematic issues keep repeating themselves, but then you've got issues anyway. It might be that some of them are not immediately solvable, because you've got the same squad for Tuesday because of injuries, but you can talk up how well certain players have done in the circumstances and that everyone wants to do well by the club, while still conceding that the performance wasn't good enough. People aren't idiots. Managers need help; they need second opinions.

Roberto Martínez was a nightmare in this regard at Everton. We'd lose 3–0 and he'd say we'd played really well, or that we'd kept the ball really well. It was a pile of shite, to be honest. There's a key difference between positivity and pie-in-the-sky stuff, and that difference is credibility. If you don't try and educate yourself on your knowledge gaps, you lose credibility on a topic. And in this scenario, that lack of credibility leads to the crowd losing faith. This quickly filters down to the players, because you become worried that the manager isn't being honest with you or the supporters.

The rise of sports psychologists and the potential riches that the modern game provides make it easier for players to be driven towards success – both individual and shared – but the principal conclusion is that motivation isn't something you can fake easily. You can be urged on by supporters, family, agents, psychologists and coaches, and some of them might even be able to shape your personality. But eventually it comes down to the individual, and if someone just isn't as determined to succeed as they could be, football is an unforgiving and ultra-competitive world in which to make your living. There's always someone ready to take your place, and always a younger model coming through.

Motivation

by Anne-Marie Silbiger

Do not fret
Breathe deep
Move forward
Growth is ours

8

RACISM

*'Nobody is born a racist; people learn to
be racist. If you can learn something,
you can unlearn it too.'*
Show Racism the Red Card

It's very hard for me to talk about racism, because I simply can't get my head around treating someone differently because of the colour of their skin. I think at its heart it is pure tribalism: you're different, so we believe that you're going to hurt us – and therefore you're the enemy. But that viewpoint is utterly ridiculous.

I find it bizarre that a few decades ago certain players would have been abused and taunted on a daily, hourly basis for daring to strive to be successful in their field, just because people look at others not for who they are and how they behave but what they look like. What difference does the colour of someone's skin make? It's mad. I'm watching the football on TV, and I'm not thinking, 'Oh, that player's black'; they're just footballers, and some might look different to others. Who bloody cares?

I remember playing against Liverpool when John Barnes had bananas thrown at him. It was a disgrace, quite obviously. But for Barnes, the good thing was that the more you abused him, the better he played. He used it as fuel to teach the racists a lesson, which is extraordinary when you actually think about it. The strength of character that must have taken is remarkable.

As a footballer – or at least, this is the case for almost every footballer – you have respect for every player as a person, whether they're on your team or not. You don't want to see anyone going through that. You looked at the people doing it, and you just thought that if that's the people they are – and either they think this is acceptable or they don't care that it isn't – they shouldn't be anywhere near the ground in the first place. I don't think anyone was on their side.

But one thing that did happen was that the abuse of Barnes and others was too quickly forgotten. We played the game, we saw what happened, but we moved on to the next game. There was no huge reaction from us as players because we had to think about the next matches. It was easy for us white players to move on, but what about those who suffered the abuse?

Black players today owe so much to the likes of Barnes, Clyde Best, Cyrille Regis, Viv Anderson and others, because they were the ones who came through and bore the brunt of the abuse but who were strong enough to keep going and resolved that they wouldn't let the racists win. And they did so without the support network within the game that's in place now. They created a platform for those who followed them, and they changed opinion through their strength, their perseverance and their quality.

These players normalised the fact that black players featured at the top level of the game, and so others were able to come through and follow their example. Their legacy is the comparative – and I stress the word 'comparative' – lack of abuse that black players suffer today. But while we rightly celebrate their impact as pioneers, we should also apologise deeply to them that they suffered such abuse. The game itself should have led the way, not these players.

Of course, society was different then. We were fed misinformation by the written media and on TV and radio. You look back now at how black people were portrayed on telly in the 1970s and it makes you cringe. If you go to a charity dinner these days and a comedian tells a racist joke, it's completely unacceptable. But it's not that long since that stuff was deemed OK.

It's also clear that some people still feel that way, although thankfully they're a small minority. They see people through the prism of their ingrained racism, and judge them by different standards because of the colour of their skin. That some of them also feel empowered to express those beliefs is a damning indictment of our society.

Racism is learnt behaviour. Nobody is born inherently racist. But an acceptance of racism is created by the environment people grow up in. If in your household it's deemed acceptable to treat people differently because of the colour of their skin, you might well become hardened to behave that way too. But I believe that this can change, because society has shifted. If you can learn to be racist, you can also learn not to be racist.

Unfortunately, that educational process is threatened by the behaviour of people at the very top of society, and their rhetoric and policies actively work against minorities. It reminds me of a *Carry On* film, in that these people can apparently say whatever they want because it's all a joke to them, and as long as they say it's a joke they can repeatedly get away with it.

Boris Johnson is like Sid James. He says something offensive, but it's all OK because it was just a harmless joke. Fine, but you tell that to the child who's crying at school because he's being treated differently because he looks different. You tell that to the people who are abused in the street or on a train or at work because they've been identified as the enemy. You tell that to a fella who has had to leave his wife and kids because he's being deported. See if that 'good old Boris' image holds up then. But he continues to get his way. People are fools, because he's supposed to be there for us not us there for him. And if he isn't producing a society we want, he has to go.

In the middle of the coronavirus pandemic, the government announced that those with expiring work visas would be allowed to stay on to help with the crisis. That really annoyed me as it just revealed the government's agenda. You can stay here for as long as we consider you useful, carrying out incredible, life-saving work while we need you. And then when it's done, we'll tell you to leave. How's that for gratitude? They will allow them to stay for as long as it's popular for them to stay – after all, it would be a huge political own goal to get rid of any NHS workers during a pandemic. But as soon as it becomes popular to victimise and lambast those same people again, they'll turn on them. You'll hear the same group of politicians attacking the very people who deserve gratitude. If the crisis has taught us anything, it's that we simply don't have the skills in this country to cope on our own.

In the background you have people like Nigel Farage, who just takes the piss. He spouts all the time about how bad Europe is, but doesn't forget to pick up his £83,000 salary a year. And yet he's won the game he's playing. He could do anything and people would just double down on their support for his principles. And don't get me started on Tommy Robinson, with his massive house and grounds.

But very few people see through all this. Is the country that bad that we think this is the answer, with the people at the top just looking after themselves, and those at the bottom left hoping for a few scraps? And yet the media continue to back them and sell all this as a positive future for the country. It's absolutely scandalous.

We often hear the 'freedom of speech' argument from those who use racial slurs, but there's a difference between free speech and hate speech. If you have friends who are black, Asian or from minority ethnic (BAME) groups, there might be an understanding between you, because you know each other, where you can take the piss out of each other. But when you say anything outside of the boundaries of that under-standing then you have a moral and legal responsibility to avoid certain slurs. You can't hide behind the 'You can't say anything these days' defence, because it's nonsense. You can say anything, as long as it isn't racially hurtful or offensive. And you don't get to choose what is and isn't racially offen-sive. That isn't the right of the person saying it.

One of the most damaging consequences of racism is that it forced people into their shells. Some of those who became famous were afraid to be proud of their ethnic heritage, of their identity, because they realised that the only way they could be accepted was to try to fit in. They were having to hide who they were in plain sight, and that's a crime on the part of the society in which they lived. Those who did come through, be it in football or in any other industry, deserve to be celebrated forever. You cannot overstate the courage and strength of mind it took for them to get where they got to, with a heavy boot constantly placed on their heads trying to push them down.

I know there's a certain section of society that worries about a 'takeover' by a different culture, but honestly you have to ask what their thought process is. Culture evolves, and it always has done. Things might be different in ten years' time, just like they were different ten, twenty and thirty years ago – that's because a society isn't set in stone. It's a melting pot and the ingredients constantly change. That's a beautiful thing, not a reason to be fearful.

Treating or judging anyone on the basis of the colour of their skin is ludicrous. Either you're good enough to do a job or you're not. Either you're a good footballer or you're not. And putting roadblocks in the way of any section of society based on anything other than their suitability for a task is unacceptable. That should be spectacularly obvious, and so it is to lots of people. But that it even needs saying shows how far we still have to go.

We always hear the line about football only reflecting society, and of course there's some truth to that. But football could also choose to lead the way. Nothing both simultaneously excites so many people and brings so many people together in one place like football, not even religion. But the game has got to want to do it. It has to want to eradicate racism as much as it wants to make money. And unfortunately we've got a game with debased, or deprioritised, morals.

It needs someone to get the Premier League clubs together and say, 'This is how it's going to be. We're going to lead the fight against racism by fully eradicating it from our game. Forget those in society who wish to divide us and aggravate racial hatred, because we're going to fight against them.' There has to be a mandate.

Fans racially abuse players because of their own ignorance – and often because they're drunk – and it's based on the idea we looked at in a previous chapter that abuse is somehow acceptable within football stadiums. I wish fans would feel that they could stand up to others, and this relates to the overall environment that has been created at the club. If you believe that the club cares about you – and so you care about the club – fans might be more prepared to call out those who cross the line.

If fans display racist behaviour, your club should be docked points if it is shown not to have banned the guilty parties for life. If there is proof of racism within your squad, players must be sacked and no other club in the country can sign them until they have demonstrated that they've educated themselves as to why their behaviour was abhorrent. Football only gets to use societal racism as an excuse if it has done everything within its own power to stamp it out.

* * *

The next step for black, Asian and ethnic minorities in English football is for the progression of coaches and managers. We hear from so many coaches and managers from these communities who lament the lack of opportunities they've been afforded, having either been turned down for interviews or gone to numerous interviews and never been given a chance. I read somewhere that 25 per cent of the professional players in this country are BAME, but only 3 per cent of the managers. This has to indicate that something has gone wrong somewhere.

There are very few clubs who want to take a chance on a young BAME coach, and the knock-on effect of that is that retiring BAME players, who may be wealthy as a result of their career in the game, probably think that it isn't worth the bother. They might already have seen how the environment is skewed against them, so they understandably shy away from it.

But this isn't just about the future of individual stakeholders – players, coaches, referees, fans, even individual governing bodies. Football on a global scale needs to take responsibility too. Why did we ever go to the World Cup in Russia? What example does that set? I think we should have sent a gay team and given the message to Vladimir Putin that this is what we think about his country's treatment of the LGBTQ+ community.

Why are we allowing a World Cup to take place in Qatar, where homosexuality is illegal and punishable with up to three years in prison? The Qatari government fails to recognise same-sex marriage, and does not allow for any public campaigning for LGBTQ+ rights. Minorities continue to face structural racism and the treatment of migrant workers has been appalling. A supposedly universal and inclusive sport taking its flagship tournament there shows how wrapped up in politics and money the game has become. I've no issue with football being economically successful, but not at the expense of the liberties of other people.

Both UEFA and FIFA have all the backbone of a jellyfish. They should come down hard on any form of racism, and if that means throwing teams out of competitions rather than just issuing small fines or forcing games behind closed doors, then that's what must happen. If you want to behave like that, so be it. But you won't play in our competitions anymore, and you won't get our funding. The national governing bodies would soon start taking the issue seriously. But they won't do it. They don't want the challenge or the publicity.

I worry deeply that FIFA, UEFA and the Football Association are just playing at all this. They have to do something about the rise of racism, but – other than wearing some T-shirts – it all seems so reactive. What can we actually do to alter society so that these problems don't keep happening? This is football, a game that's supposed to have the power to change the world. But we've allowed it to become a sanitised version of itself.

Things will eventually improve, I'm sure of that. We're already at a place where any racist abuse or mistreatment is widely lambasted by the football community and the presence of BAME players has become normalised, and these are hugely positive things. The appointment of coaches and managers at the top level will hopefully follow. Football has the power to rail against ingrained racism in politics and in society, and I hope that it recognises that power and utilises it.

But football – and ourselves – can never take our eye off the ball, because racism festers and multiplies when it lies unchecked and untreated. If English football is to pride itself on its universality and stand as a testament to our multiculturalism, the fight against the bastards that are intent on dividing us and pursuing their belief that white is best should never cease.

Racism

by Anne-Marie Silbiger

One person struggles, another person relaxes
Privilege in their hands, unearned
Why do we strive to be just
In a body fully equipped to love?

9

HOMOPHOBIA

'LGBTQ+ people don't pose a threat to others,
but people's ignorance and hatred does cause
a threat towards LGBTQ+ people.'
TransActual UK

The first thing to say, and it's important to make this point, is that there are gay footballers in the men's professional game. Given statistics and probability, there have to be. There are just no *openly* gay footballers in the men's game.

It's important here to make a distinction between the men's and the women's game. Women's football welcomes and cherishes gay players, and they have become influential role models for openly gay supporters. That's brilliant. But I'm also sure that the women's game is acutely aware that the more popular it gets, and the more people go to watch the games, the more the chances increase of knobheads going to watch it. Nobody can rest on their laurels. A rise in popularity brings with it both positive and negative impacts. The plus is that more people will watch women's football, and the negative is that more bigots will be tempted to air their views about it. Every sport has that.

There's obviously an array of different reasons why nobody

has yet felt able to come out in the men's professional game. First, it comes down to the individual: what type of person they are, what's going on in their private life, whether their family are aware of their sexuality. But there's a huge lack of trust on the part of gay players, and I completely understand that. If you're going to come out as a professional, perhaps even elite-level, footballer, you're going to open yourself up to a huge amount of unknown impacts. And the unknown is always scary. That's a huge amount to deal with for anyone, particularly someone who might have struggled privately with their sexual preference.

Then there's the environment in which players operate. I'm fully aware that a football dressing room is a lot less macho and testosterone-filled than it used to be, but that climate does still exist to an extent. I think the fear about football's 'macho' identity concerns the pitch more than the dressing room. There would be a fear that opponents might use the fact that you are gay against you, however unacceptable that would be. When I went into a dressing room with fifteen or so other people, I certainly didn't care which players were black, foreign, gay, whatever; they were my teammates. They were all Everton and we were all Everton. All I cared about was whether they were going to let me down on the pitch or help us win things. It didn't matter a jot to me who they were, and I honestly believe the same is true of all the players I shared the dressing room with.

One problem was that nobody talked about gay players back then. In our dressing room, and in my hometown, nobody even considered it as a possibility and nobody thought to raise it as a topic of conversation. And that sent a message to anyone who might be scared of coming out that they were best keeping quiet about it, as well as suggesting to them that they didn't belong there. Everybody was close-minded and scared of sharing their feelings, and perhaps in some respects football still suffers from this problem. As players, we talked about the match or going out on the town, but we didn't talk about our personal lives. That made it very hard for someone to bring sensitive stuff into the dressing room, particularly if they were wrestling with something like coming out. I can see why it didn't happen.

I think it's easy to say that football dressing rooms wouldn't welcome an openly gay footballer, but I also think it's inaccurate. Where do people who make such a claim get this information? And how do they know that this is what non-openly gay players are fearful of? The clubs in which I operated would certainly have been OK with it. I think it's an easy way of absolving other parties – governing bodies, particularly – of guilt in failing to create an environment in which a gay player feels comfortable enough to come out. It judges football on the basis of the 1970s and 1980s, but we no longer apply such old-fashioned standards to people who present TV programmes, to take one example. And football has evolved too.

The only real way to dispel the myth of the homophobic dressing room is to find out. Go to every club and contact every player through the Professional Footballers' Association (PFA) and ask them if they'd have a problem with a gay player in the dressing room, whether they'd welcome and support him. And then use that data to make a statement saying that 100 per cent (hopefully) of players at each level would back and support a gay teammate. In this scenario, every player in the club would be committed to creating a positive environment. Every player that signed the statement would be named and would be proud to put their name to it. This would go a long way towards creating a climate of acceptance. If there were players that refused to sign, they should be invited to attend educational sessions in which their views could be challenged and their prejudices examined to try to improve their worldview and make them more tolerant people.

That isn't to say that there isn't a culture of taking the piss that exists within dressing rooms. On the training ground in my day, if someone had a big nose or had big ears, that would be picked up on in the to and fro of friendly banter. And that's before 'banter' became twisted to mean something that it never used to. But if we knew that a player was struggling with something, we'd have helped them rather than the opposite. We didn't slaughter our mates because we didn't like them; it was just something that happened and still continues to happen inside and outside of football. You're close enough that there's a circle of trust not to take things too far, but you all took the piss out of each other.

I think part of that was testing a player's mettle, because if you couldn't survive in the dressing room or on the training ground, then you were likely to struggle on the pitch, where opponents were prepared to do it ten times worse and they weren't your friends. It's certainly true to say that there's a fine line between testing the mettle of someone that you know and bullying, and you have to get that right. I don't agree with the stuff that sometimes used to happen with apprentices, and the idea of initiation rituals, at Everton and at most other clubs.

I remember in pre-season that Howard Kendall would have us training until 11.45am, and then he'd get the goal out and tell the apprentices to stand on the line. Their job was to stop all the balls going into the net. We would all smash the ball at them and be rolling around laughing, and we treated it as a bit of fun. But what about the apprentices themselves? You cannot do that now, and rightly so. There was a lack of awareness at that time about how such behaviour could affect players, even if in Howard's head it was done for reasons of squad morale. That's not how you treat people, and there are better ways to strengthen players, although it's very easy to look back in hindsight and criticise. It was shit, but then progress always involves a series of stepping stones of improvement. If it looks shit now, at least things have changed.

We have to do as much work as possible within academies to ensure that the next generation of players are educated fully on certain issues. Players have so much time to fill that there really isn't any excuse not to. You need to have a full programme of learning on issues such as racism, homophobia and transphobia.

I went into a primary school in Merthyr Tydfil, just outside the Brecon Beacons, as part of the Show Racism the Red Card initiative, where we spoke about how unacceptable it was to use the N-word. One of the kids responded by saying that their dad used the word at home, so we asked them whether they thought that was acceptable, given what they'd heard. In response, the kid said, 'Yes, I don't see the problem. Who cares?' Only through education can we ensure that such regressive attitudes are addressed at the earliest possible opportunity. That's why the work is so important.

But generally speaking, young people now are so much more liberal in their views, and they deserve credit for this. I see first-hand that most of them don't care about people's sexuality or skin colour like some adults do – that a whole spectrum of variety is more normal to them and they're comfortable talking about such things. This creates a better environment, as hiding something makes it seem as if you should be ashamed of it. It's certainly unacceptable that we've made any gay person in this country feel like they cannot come out if they want to.

Part of the problem is the blurred line between 'banter' and abuse, and the mistakes people make when drawing that line. All I hear now is that you can't say a word to anyone 'these days' for fear of causing offence or upsetting them, implying that nobody can take a joke. But that's simply not true. It just depends upon your relationship with them. You hear gay people talking to each other, and if they're close then they might use the word 'fag' or 'queer' in a jokey context. But that doesn't mean that straight people or gay people they don't know can call them that, because in that scenario the word takes on a different, loaded meaning. The onus is on you to avoid offending, not on people to avoid being offended. The fault lies with you. Anything else is victim-blaming.

I do think that it comes down to having an attitude in Britain that's unique to us, and it isn't a good thing. We think that because we once administered a large portion of the world this gives us the right to treat people in a certain way, as if they should somehow be subservient to us and fall into line with everything we say. We're British, we'll say what we want – and if you don't like it, then go somewhere else. But we didn't rule the world; we ruined it. What we did in various parts of the world was disgusting when you look back at it. But we perpetuate the imperial attitude because it makes us feel good about ourselves. There's us, and then below us everyone else. Our history as a country means that we should be atoning for it by treating other people better, not worse.

Our colonial mindset led to our backward treatment of difference. When I was growing up, communities were small. Anyone that was different – gay, bisexual, mentally ill, whatever – was considered to be 'dodgy'. I think – or I hope – that we've come a long way since then, but that only indicates just how stupid such behaviour was in the first place and how far we still have to go. Even today, there are people who want to stop refugees coming into this country to flee war, or who might treat black or Asian people worse than people of their own colour or 'nationality'. But then they're perfectly happy to go out for a curry or a Chinese meal. They're quite content to interact with people up to the point that suits them, but *only* up to that point. And that selective attitude must stem from colonialism. We'll take what we can from you, right up until we no longer consider you to be useful to us.

For any player who might be considering being openly gay, I think the first issue is one of control. It's about giving a player the power to come out on their own terms, and in exactly the manner that makes them feel most comfortable. If you're aware, for example, that there's a tabloid media that might delight in running the story that you're gay, and either splash it on their front page or give you forty-eight hours' warning that they're going to splash it, that takes all control away from you. And it's going to make you feel uncomfortable about how you might expect to be treated by that self-same media afterwards. Serious questions also need to be asked about whether the Football Association has gone far enough in its preparations. I've never seen anyone from the FA go onto Sky Sports or BBC Sport and detail exactly what the protocol is for when a player does come out. But that should have happened. It should be public knowledge.

The FA could state beyond any doubt that they would be fully behind any player who came out. They could stipulate that there would be added security around the player for a period of time, to offer protection in case of any unacceptable backlash or media intrusion. It shouldn't be needed, but let's plan for the worst. They could name a few experts in the field of counselling who would immediately be made available to the player; this person will help the individual, this person will support the family, this person will work with individuals within the club. They could nominate someone to go into the player's club on a full-time basis to act as a go-between for player and governing body to ensure that everything they need to feel comfortable is taken care of and arrange anything that might be lacking.

They could also spell out the disciplinary action that would be taken against any incidents of homophobic abuse and the extra support that would be given to the player in such circumstances: fining clubs significant amounts of money for any abuse that came from the stands, punishing players with lengthy bans if they were proven to have directed abuse at their fellow professionals and docking their clubs points if behaviour didn't improve. The money from fines would be given to LGBTQ+ charities.

If the FA laid all of that out on national TV and in the press, it would confirm that they had proactively done everything in their power and it would send a message to all players that the national governing body had their backs. They would also be proactively casting those who abused a player as pariahs who wouldn't be welcome at the ground or club ever again. Those abusive knobheads couldn't say that they hadn't been warned.

Then the FA should initiate discussions with a number of gay fan groups and openly gay participants in other sports on the issues they encountered and feared before coming out, because only by learning from these experiences can the organisation be adequately prepared to help a footballer that came out. Their worries might not exactly match, but if you spoke to a cross-section of the community then you could be prepared for most things. You are proving to the public – and the gay community – that you are there en masse to provide a circle of support that lasts for as long as required.

It would also be crucial for the FA to pull all of the media into discussions, not to get their opinion but to tell them exactly how it would be handled, and to outline what could or could not be said. This wouldn't be about media control or hampering the free press, but about ensuring that the player was given the most positive treatment to ensure that their mental well-being is maintained. I'd hazard a guess that the worry over salacious gossip and intrusion into their private lives ranks high among the reasons why a player wouldn't want to come out – and that's completely unacceptable.

People have a responsibility, and that responsibility isn't simply to sell papers, increase audience numbers or have things shared on social media. It's about human decency.

Media organisations could also be asked to sign up to a special code of conduct that would come into effect when a player made it known to the FA or their club that they wanted to come out publicly. And any organisation that broke that code of conduct would lose their privileged access. They wouldn't be welcome at England press conferences or be given interview access to England players.

If you do all that, you're at the stage where you have everything in place and – just as importantly – everyone knows that you have everything in place. The more plans and procedures you've got, the more positive an environment you create for any non-openly gay player to become an openly gay player. Reacting is too late; it isn't enough. But right now, in the hypothetical scenario of asking a non-openly gay player if they believed that everything in everyone's power had been done to make it as easy as possible for them, I think the answer would be no. And that's wholly inexcusable.

Let's assume that a Premier League player is considering coming out. You'd time it so it happened before a home game. That way, at least 80 per cent of the ground would produce an outpouring of love, respect and support to the player for their courage. There might be comments in the privacy of people's homes, and on group chats between blokes, and I don't think you will stop that from happening. It happens already about all manner of things. We're so Victorian in our views that anything different will always cause a reaction. That's incredibly sad.

The journey might not be easy. It will certainly be hardest for the ones who lead the movement, and there will be bumps in the road. But I honestly believe that we can get there. And, unlike with black players in the 1970s, society is already further along the road with LGBTQ+ issues than football is, because there's a huge number of openly gay people in this country. So the hope is that they can skip some of the more painful stages of the process that black players had to go through.

But there will still be plenty of hurdles. By agreeing to play World Cups in Qatar and Russia, where there's such intolerance, we allow that intolerance to fester with our implicit support. The FA are inadvertently telling gay people, 'Fuck off, we don't value you.' If once in a while we said, 'Sorry, we don't agree with your approach to human rights or your inability to deal with racism or the treatment of LGBTQ+ communities in your country, so we won't be going,' imagine the boost that would give to oppressed communities. But we never do.

There's also the issue of presentation and communication. Everything should be a celebration of equality. For instance, rather than having Rainbow Laces Day and Show Racism the Red Card Day, why not have all these things happening all the time and therefore happening together? That creates a united message of equality. Why aren't the FA going to Pride and arranging that Everton play Liverpool on the same day as Merseyside Pride, thereby combining the two events? Rather than having Rainbow Laces Day on one weekend per year, as if that's as much time we can afford to campaign for gay rights, do it every game. Have the Merseyside Pride march start at one of the grounds, and have representatives walking around the pitch. It has to become normalised to see openly gay people at football matches.

We could get the Rainbow Toffees and other associated LGBTQ+ clubs to play on Premier League pitches. Doing that does two things: first, it's their dream to play at Goodison; second, it's a stepping stone to having gay footballers on the pitch as an everyday, unremarkable thing.

In short, we need to stop treating gay players as a special event. The first time it happens you might get a few twats that shout things or make a fuss, but you'll quickly be able to spot them, and over time there will be fewer and fewer of them. People will become so used to seeing gay footballers on the pitch that soon they won't give them a second glance.

These are stepping stones, of course, but they're invaluable. The players from clubs like the Rainbow Toffees are desperate to do this, and that in itself shows tremendous courage. They deserve this opportunity, and these regular stepping stones are the only way forward. At some point people have to make significant, proactive decisions on important issues rather than just reacting – let things be challenged, consult people, find out what works.

I've spoken at length about the need to have a complete framework in place to support a player that comes out, but you also have to be clever with how that framework is implemented. Because I'd imagine that any player that does come out would want to be treated exactly the same as they were before, particularly on the pitch. They don't want to be 'The Gay Footballer' but just a footballer who happens to be gay, although it will be hard to get right because that support network will be implemented because of who they are.

On the pitch, in the dressing room, on the training ground and walking down the street, they just want to be who they are without feeling different or special in any way. If they play shit, they'll be happy to get grief from the manager or opposition supporters. If they play well, they'll be happy to get exactly the same treatment as any other player. Nobody wants to be made to feel different, because that brings with it greater pressure and greater strain on their mental health. They just want to be treated the same, and all of those plans are to ensure that can happen as time passes post-announcement.

I do wish it would happen, because it would open the floodgates for other players to be themselves. But it's also not my place to demand it, and that's an important point to make. This isn't about forcing people to come out, or urging them to. It has to be on their terms, and has to be a decision based on the preference of the individual. But if we create a positive environment for them too, they'll have the control. They can make their own choices, rather than be forced down a particular route.

Homophobia

by Anne-Marie Silbiger

I do not want your attention
The shouts of heraldry misplaced as I squint
*   at the sun*
Now I hide in the dark
Waiting for empty pavements
I exist

10

ADDICTION

'I didn't even know I was addicted
until I tried to stop.'
Alan Wright
(@ScrtDrugAddict)

Playing football gives you an incredible number of highs, and each of those highs can be tremendously exhilarating. The feeling of winning an important match against a tough opponent, of scoring a goal or saving a penalty is hard to describe, but it's total elation. The buzz in those moments is extraordinary. Just think about how it would feel to stand on the steps of the town hall, or on an open-top bus, and have tens of thousands of people chanting your name. It makes you feel untouchable. It feels like nothing else.

But the consequence of this is there's nothing that can ever reproduce such feelings. If I was about to pull off a great save at Goodison, I could actually hear the crowd hold its breath … and then release it when the save was made. How can you possibly replicate that? And how could it fail to be addictive?

One option is to just take your mind off the need to feel that buzz. When I was playing, we probably had more outlets to find a release. Players went to the pub and had a few beers, or went on team days to the races. They were able to get their release in a non-managed environment. But that isn't as easy now.

The money doesn't help either, because money can't buy that same buzz that you feel on the pitch. You buy a Ferrari and drive it fast today, you buy a Lamborghini tomorrow; nothing really changes. It's a futile search to re-create that buzz. High wages just mean you spend more money trying to find it.

Then there's the free time footballers are afforded. You train for a few hours a day, but the rest of the time is your own, and you're actively advised not to do anything too strenuous. You can't go away for a few days because you've got training the next day. You can't take on any long-term projects like business ventures because you don't want to lose any focus. You might end up going shopping or watching films or playing golf, but there are so many hours in the day to fill.

When you know that the best moment of your week, in terms of excitement and buzz, will come at a certain time on a Saturday, all the other days can lose their meaning. Some of them can seem incredibly quiet by comparison, and it can be hard to mentally manage the vast difference between the highs and lows.

The hardest thing – and the impossible thing for some players – is to try to fill your time and entertain yourself without succumbing to the bad habits that everyone knows can provide artificial highs. I didn't see any drugs when I was in the game; honestly, never, not once. It just didn't seem to be a thing, although I'm sure a few people just kept it well hidden.

A few smoked, but that wasn't really a widespread thing, because even then people realised that it wasn't good for your fitness.

Alcohol was different. Drinking has ruined more than a few people, and you can see how it happens. Alcohol enables players to move out of themselves, to relieve the pressure and find some escape, giving them a chemical high that can become addictive. It's a social tool that, in the wrong hands, turns into an anti-social crutch.

We had a young midfielder at Everton who had come through the club's academy. As soon as we saw him play as a youngster, we knew he was special. His passing range was brilliant, but he also had that hunger and energy that all the best players seem to have. Peter Beardsley compared him to Paul Gascoigne, and I think he was right.

But he just struggled to handle the pressures of being a footballer. He got a nasty injury that ruled him out for a few months, and without the structure of training every day he began the descent into alcohol and substance abuse. I think he fell in with the wrong crowd and started drinking with people who were just hanging around him because he was a footballer. We only really found out about that after the event, and I never saw it, but he got addicted to cocaine and started missing training regularly. Everton tried to send him to a clinic to get straightened out, but eventually he left the club. He played his last professional game at 21. It's amazing how quickly decline sets in once you go down the wrong path.

But gambling was the most notorious addiction that foot-ballers suffered from, and I'm sure it still is. There was an awful lot of gambling that I witnessed as a player. Footballers had so much time on their hands, they had a decent disposable income, they could bet easily on things that they were interested in anyway and it helped to create a buzz similar to the one they experienced on the pitch.

I think a lot of players considered gambling to be a perfectly acceptable way of finding that high, even if they realised that it was addictive. It didn't replace the buzz of scoring a goal, but it did give them their best chance of mimicking it. Whether it was betting on horses, betting on a game of golf, pool or cards with each other or betting on two flies running up a wall, it didn't matter. It was about the thrill of the uncertainty, the financial risk and getting one over on their mates.

There were always big gamblers in each club, but there were also players who could take it or leave it. Some people just have more addictive personalities than others; it can take over their lives before they even realise. That's just the way their minds are wired. For example, I listened to Paul Merson talk about the amount of money he lost, and it's a frightening amount. You just wish that there had been more support for him at the time. It's the same with Tony Adams, who has been incredibly brave and honest when discussing his battles with alcohol abuse. Thankfully, both have come through it, but it's heart-breaking that there weren't people within the club that could have seen it early enough or been there for them to talk to.

But at the time, people just hadn't woken up to the dangers of addiction. Nobody really spoke about them. People were often described as 'a drinker' or 'a gambler', but nobody really challenged them on it or tried to offer them support. Everyone just let everyone else get on with their thing and assumed that they would talk if they wanted to stop.

You also have to remember that nearly every footballer is incredibly competitive – they've had to be to get where they are. Scouts and coaches love to see a talented player, but they love just as much seeing a player with a huge will to win and a competitive edge. When you're taught that the only focus should be on winning the next match, you can see how players become overcompetitive. The problem shows up because you can't just turn that competitive edge off and then turn it back on come the next Saturday morning. It becomes a part of you. And then the competitiveness itself, as well as the buzz, becomes addictive. You want to test yourself, whether it's on a football pitch or being able to win at cards or golf or pick the right horses and beat the bookies.

It becomes a particular danger for injured players. At least when you're playing you have the knowledge that in a few days you're likely to get another chance to experience the buzz. But when you're out of the team for a long period, and you know that your teammates are still getting that buzz and you aren't, it can be very hard to fill the days. That sense of emptiness inevitably lends itself to things like gambling.

And then when you retire, it's worse still. It isn't a huge surprise that a number of former players have opened up about their gambling addictions. If you've been used to having a bet as a player to get a buzz, and then the Saturday afternoons stop and football's no longer there to satisfy your craving, it's not hard to see how you might use gambling to fill the void. Unfortunately, when you retire you haven't got the same disposable income that you had before, and yet people find it extremely difficult to reduce their stakes. Add in the obvious increase in free time, particularly if there's a break between playing football and starting something new, and it can become a big problem. And if gambling also creates unwanted financial pressures, you can see how mental health issues can get worse.

The principle probably remains the same from when I was playing to the present day. Players are obviously paid far more money nowadays, but then that just means their stakes increase. For gambling to give people a buzz, the stakes have to be worthwhile. The risk creates the rush. A modern player just isn't going to put a fiver on a horse if he's a real gambler.

The lack of that Saturday buzz combines with a feeling of worthlessness that many former players suffer. They've grown accustomed to 30,000 people shouting their name and the close-knit environment of a dressing room. Now nobody is shouting their name and they've lost that close group of colleagues. It can make them feel, 'I was there and now I'm here. I was once a somebody and now I'm not.' In my day, players could find another job, driving a truck or running a pub or working on a building site, but very few jobs provide the same buzz as football. If you reach your destination when driving a truck, does it feel the same as scoring a goal? I don't think so. It's easy to see how you might end up doing more of the drinking or gambling to compensate for what you've lost.

All you want to do is try to help those people, but it's so hard because they have grown up, played and lived at a time when neither drinking nor gambling were seen as a problem.

Added to that, they'd also been taught that to admit a problem is to reveal your weakness, making it a perfect storm. But things have thankfully changed – communication being seen as a positive rather than a negative thing is one of the greatest leaps forward we've made in mental health, from my dad's generation to mine to today.

Luckily that old Everton teammate found a new partner, and the last few times I've seen him he looks a lot better. Maybe he just needed a better support network in his life to manage him through the process. You can see why he wouldn't want to talk about it with an old teammate – it needed the right person. You worry about people like that and their direction after football. The PFA would have helped him, but only if he sought their assistance. And he was never going to ask. I'd spoke to him a hundred times and he always insisted that he didn't have a problem – it's so hard.

The support networks just didn't exist when I was playing, but the culture was totally different too. I've seen every player get hammered on the coach on the way home from a match, play cards for money, and then jump into their cars and drive home. Society saw things in a different light then, or didn't see them at all. The culture was that the men used to go out and drink beer at the weekend. It was accepted as part of them winding down.

I think coping with retirement is more difficult when you've been in football all your life. It might have seemed like hard work at the time, but I'm so grateful that I didn't start living life as a footballer until I was twenty. My experience of other jobs meant that I knew what was coming and could mentally prepare for it. I didn't mind that work and life before I played, so I felt exactly the same at the other end of my career. But without that preparation, it must be hard. It makes you worry about the players that have gone through the academy system since the age of seven or eight, and have little concept of life outside football. How on earth do they acclimatise to the real world when they finish playing?

The adjustment is made that much harder because there really isn't any in-between support. When you're off ill in other industries, you might do a managed return to work, but that doesn't happen to a footballer, then or now. You stop playing one day, and, unless you're very fortunate to pick up coaching or media work immediately, you wake up the following day and suddenly you're not a footballer anymore. That shock to the system can be monumentally hard.

I think clubs should look at ways of getting their players into other businesses. They should have links with certain organisations. It sounds silly, but there's no job centre or careers officers for footballers. The PFA do their bit, as they did before, but in the main their hands are tied. There aren't enough bodies to get around everyone.

There's also the problem that most footballers are hard-wired not to ask for help. A footballer has a certain level of pride. They've become so used to focusing on getting themselves prepared, without the help of psychologists or hands-on management, that they feel uneasy about asking for outside help. That only pushes them further into themselves, isolating them and leaving them more prone to mental health issues.

One of the direct consequences of the more intense media spotlight on today's footballers is that it persuades players not to go out. Why would you, if someone is going to be following you with a long lens, taking photos of you to sell to a newspaper and making it a story? That doesn't make them any more likely to develop an addiction, but it does mean that if they're going to go down that road they'll do it within the four walls of their own home. If they were out on the piss, questions might be asked. But medicate yourself at home and who's going to find out?

They're also unlikely to admit that they have a problem with any addiction when they're still playing. Doing so would be viewed as a sign of weakness, and they might be concerned about being dropped from the team or losing their transfer value. You can imagine what an agent might do – they'd just cover it up. That's when I go back to the role of the FA. It really shouldn't be seen as a weakness to reveal a problem with gambling or alcohol; quite the opposite. It's a sign of strength that you've identified and addressed your problems and feel that you want to talk to someone and ask for help. The weakness is in hiding it. That message has to be pushed harder.

I'm one of the lucky ones. I've never drunk, I've never smoked and I don't bet, so I wasn't compromised by those problems. I suppose that I was very unusual at the time, but I never really gave it a moment's thought. I didn't give a fuck about anything but playing football. In that respect, maybe hard work was my addiction. Towards the end I made sure that I was at the training ground by 7am. I'd have a bath, do some weights, go and have my breakfast, do some gym work and then go out with some of the lads who'd arrived early. After training, I might play some head tennis with a few of them, then go back to the gym and have some late lunch before going home. When I got back I'd do as little as possible. I'd done my work, so I just sat and read or watched TV. Having a rest became part of the working process.

The biggest connection between addiction and footballers is the game's relationship with the gambling industry. You turn on the TV and it's all you see. Professional leagues in this country are sponsored by bookmakers. Half the clubs in the Premier League have gambling sponsors plastered on the front of their shirts. What message does that send?

The FA are the game's governing body. They have to try to do more to avoid this unfortunate situation, because players' problems with their gambling addiction can only have been made worse by the close relationship between the two industries. You can't just tell players that they can't do certain things, and then sit back and be happy that you've solved the issue. You haven't; you've just made it go underground. The FA simply has to create an open dialogue with players and clubs about gambling.

But football lost its morals a long time ago. The game's there to make money, and that's it. No other reason. And when you put football into that context, of course it has tied itself closely to gambling – and has been happy to do so – because dancing that particular dance makes it money. A lot of money.

There's no doubt that many people are able to use gambling as a form of fun and entertainment without it becoming a huge problem, either in terms of addiction or financial loss. But there's also no doubt that for some people, those with a certain type of personality, the habit quickly and devastatingly becomes unmanageable.

I think the rise in gambling came with the vast increase in televised sport and the dawn of the internet age. You'd have people that might put a bet on if they went to the football on a Saturday who suddenly had an infinite choice of matches to watch and things to gamble on. Because bookmakers are guaranteed to make money, and because they know gambling adverts work, they flood sports coverage with their wares. I hate it when you watch a match on the TV, and every ad break is full of offers to do with betting. At the end of these adverts they have a little message: 'Please bet responsibly.' As if that's going to work. No gambling addict or potential gambling addict has ever been influenced by that message in any way.

One of the things that really annoyed me during the coronavirus crisis was noticing the continuing number of gambling adverts on TV. I think that's disgusting, because it's simply an organised form of preying on the vulnerable. I think the government should have banned adverts for gambling and loans until the crisis was over. Then they could have had a proper look at it. People are sitting at home and they see an online bingo advert and they think, 'Oh, it's only a fiver.' Then by the following week they might have spent hundreds of pounds. This country – and its government – has a duty of care to the mental health of its population, and gambling addiction has to come under it.

For all the people who are recovering addicts, the phase when they were going through their addiction was a horrible time. I speak from time to time to a girl who has battled against eating disorders, and she said that she has found it very hard because she has so much time on her hands, and that can allow the negative, damaging thoughts to become all-encompassing again.

We have to bring in measures, whether it's limiting stakes, limiting the number of bets people can place, banning gambling in sporting stadiums, banning adverts, putting in place greater scrutiny of how much people are spending or just increasing the funding to help those with addiction problems. I know some people would kick up a fuss and say that it infringes on their pleasure, but when you see the damage that's done to people's lives, it's hard to argue against. But it's an incredibly hard issue to solve, because the danger is that it all just goes underground.

Why has it taken so long to enforce bans on gambling in football, when everyone knows that it causes severe addiction problems and some of the best players in the English game have succumbed to it? Why did it take people lobbying the FA to persuade them to avoid gambling sponsorships? Money. And that matters most to them. Yet that's not what a governing body should be. I get it – they give you £2 million and it helps the game. But then it also makes it very hard for them to come out and claim that they care about gambling and addiction and other issues too.

I was at Wembley for the first ever Just a Ball Game? conference. There were seminars on LGBTQ+ issues within football, and they wanted to hold it at the home of the English game. But they were charged by the FA to host it there. Now don't you think that the FA, given the subject material and how much they say they are committed to these issues, might have waived the fee? People were speaking out about the abuse and treatment they've received within the game, urging improvements at every level. Was it really worth taking that money off them when they have such an important mission?

I think the FA care about the image of the game, then about having the money to sustain that image, then about the very top of the sport, then everything else. But just caring about the image isn't enough; there has to be more behind it. A high-profile incident happens, and they rush to condemn it and say that everyone must be better – but that's only words – and then it dies down. It has to be an ongoing, deeper process. Because eventually, if left unsolved, the dance with the gambling industry will destroy the image of the sport.

Gambling threatens to get worse before it gets better. With the rise of online betting, the increased money in the game, the media intrusion, the scrutiny by the public and on social media, and the abuse of players, it leads to players being more vulnerable to addiction, which in turn threatens to create a mental health epidemic among footballers. If the game hasn't learnt that yet, it never will. But I also think that the conversation around addiction needs to change in this country. We have a blame culture that pins addiction on those that suffer from it, as if they have somehow chosen to suffer. Someone might choose to place a bet or have a drink, but they do not choose addiction. It becomes an all-conquering force that takes over lives and ruins them.

It comes down to embracing things from outside your own experience. If you cannot see anything that lies outside your frame of reference, and you have never suffered from addiction, addicts can seem like weak people or maybe somehow to be blamed for their struggles. But if you can remember to have some empathy, it puts addiction into the same realm as someone struggling with mental health issues, something deserving of help not censure. Addicts deserve a society that has a framework in place to help them on their road to recovery, not one loaded against them.

Addiction

by Anne-Marie Silbiger

This road of twists and turns
Beaten paths calling your name
Monsters leaping out at random
Ready to watch you fall

11

ALCOHOL

'Recovery is not a race. You don't have to feel guilty
if it takes you longer than you thought it would.'
Alan Wright
(@ScrtDrugAddict)

The first time I met Howard Kendall was when Everton made an approach to sign me and I'd been driven to the club to agree terms on a contract. His first words when I went in to meet him was to ask me if I wanted a drink. That was just the way things were done. When I told him that I was teetotal, he looked at me in total disbelief. He couldn't believe that a footballer might not like to have a drink. I was the weird one.

After I signed the contract, he wanted to go out on the town with me and get pissed, which I presumed was a normal routine with new signings. He showed me a few places in the city and he drank in each of them, still not quite believing or understanding that I wasn't into alcohol. But he didn't try to force it on me or anything. I just had a few steaks while he had his drinks.

I was a naturally shy person. I kept myself to myself at Bury, and the same thing happened at Everton. Nobody really took me under their wing, and my shyness meant that it took quite a long time before anyone really got to know me. I think if I had been a drinker then I probably would have settled in quicker with the other players. It meant that I didn't go out with them to the pub or nightclubs, which they considered to be team-bonding exercises. They probably thought I was a loner because I didn't want to get pissed with them.

Even so, I don't think Howard ever really understood me not drinking. After the first couple of times he asked and I said no, he left me alone. But when I'd been at the club for a few years he would occasionally offer me a beer. By that stage I could tell him to fuck off as a joke. He had a Lucozade bottle that he used to fill with whisky and lemonade, and he offered me some of that. I just told him that I really didn't need it.

To be honest, I think I was probably an exception for Howard because he didn't seem to trust people who didn't drink. For him it was a crucial part of socialising and team morale, and those who didn't do it were putting that morale at risk. But it never came between us. He knew I wasn't doing it to be awkward; it just wasn't my thing and it didn't do anything for me. And I wasn't judging anyone who did it.

It was unusual to not drink as a professional footballer at that time, but I can't say that anyone really cared too much about me being teetotal. They were too busy getting on with their own lives. They let me do my thing and I let them do theirs, and I was never treated differently because of it. In fact, some of them were very happy with me not being a drinker because it meant that if we went out for a team meal, I wouldn't be drunk, so I could drive and give them a lift home.

But I should also say that their drinking never bothered me either. I never thought differently of them for drinking – it was just something that nearly everybody did. If we played away from home a long way from Liverpool, we might have a five-hour drive back after the game. They all drank beer, got pissed, fell asleep – and we still had two hours left. So I just watched a film on the TV.

When I played, I honestly don't think the players understood the potential negative impacts of alcohol. In terms of performance, at one point it was so prevalent in English football that it didn't really ever become a factor because everyone was doing the same thing. That's not to say that the players were pissed every day, because that simply wasn't the case. But they valued the social aspect of it, and so did the managers. It was used as a method of team-bonding, and you can see why it would help with that. Even now in businesses across the world, nights out are arranged between colleagues where everyone lets their hair down. So if any manager came into a club and tried to stamp it out during that era, he'd have struggled to do so. Alex Ferguson managed it to some extent at Manchester United, but even that took until the 1990s.

Digging deeper, I think that in the absence of sports psychologists, plenty of players used alcohol as a coping mechanism and a release. That's the way they saw it. They'd play the game, have a few beers, have a night out and then start all over again. That was their best way of processing what had happened and releasing the tension that built up to perform on the pitch. And that's probably still the same for lots of people in society now. You look at towns on a Friday night and you don't have to go far to see the proof.

As I say, players didn't get pissed all the time, and if they did drink they'd come in and do extra fitness work on a Monday. They weren't stupid enough to put their careers before beer, but drinking was certainly an integral part of the culture. I remember, if we were playing a team like Crystal Palace away, me, the kitman and the bus driver would go to the supermarket in the morning and buy some beers, then take the haul to the coach and fill it up. It never seemed weird at the time.

But I can see why they did it. Once you get to that level and you win a match, you can find it hard to come home – particularly after an evening kick-off. I used to get back to the house at two in the morning, and I'd be absolutely buzzing about the game. Obviously, everyone else in the house was sound asleep, so I was excited but had nobody to talk to. Their solution was to go out, get drunk and then let that send them off to sleep.

I just never even thought about drinking. It wasn't a moral decision or based on preparing for a career in football; I just don't touch the stuff. I had a sip of beer once, didn't particularly like it and so I thought, 'No, that's not for me' and that was that. Once I was playing and happy I just never thought about it, so it never really became a conscious effort. I can't ever remember thinking that I was tempted to have a drink or wanting to try something, because I was happy as I was.

It never bothered me that other people drank, and I certainly didn't judge them for it. I was just happy doing my thing and letting them do theirs. I can see why my wife Emma and our friends might want a nice glass of wine, and I can see how it might help them relax. I'm also happy to pop to the shop and buy it for them. I'll walk into Sainsbury's or Tesco, and if there isn't a bottle there that I already know, I'll just buy one based on its shape. Emma seems to like them, so I must choose OK! But I'm happy buying it – this isn't a grand moral stance. It's just that I like a nice cup of tea, and that does the same for me.

Back in the dressing room I can honestly say that I never looked at the players around me and thought that they were developing a dependence on alcohol, because a) I'm sure that most were able to leave it alone if they wanted to, and b) I don't think society really looked at social drinking in that way. In many ways, it still doesn't.

I also didn't see so much of it. We played on Saturday, I'd go home, they'd go out and get smashed. Sunday we would have off, so I didn't see them anyway. On Mondays we'd come into training, and if we'd won everyone was happy and having a laugh, and if we'd lost we would be a bit more sombre. Then Tuesday or Wednesday we often had a match, so the cycle started again. It never appeared to be a problem to me. They did what they needed to do to chill out. There were also things like end-of-season holidays, where they might have gone a little further, but I only went on one and I thought it was shit, so I never went again and never saw that side. Their idea was to have a full blow-out, and that was it. Everyone has different ways of processing things, and that was theirs.

We went on a pre-season trip to Guernsey in July 1997, and that was as bad as I saw the drinking culture. As soon as we got to the hotel, Howard filled the bar with champagne and told the lads that they were allowed to finish it. Before he left to go off and do his own thing, he told us that we all had to be in bed by midnight because we were playing a Guernsey XI the following day. He warned us that he'd send anyone home who broke the curfew.

I didn't go out, but the other lads did. The champagne was drunk and then they headed off into town. I came down the next morning and heard about the scenes that had occurred. All the players had come back to the hotel smashed, and one of the younger lads had come down in the night stark bollock naked, completely out of it, and pissed and shit himself in the lounge area of the hotel. The guy who worked behind reception took him back up to his room, washed him and tucked him back in bed. It was all a bit surreal. Howard knew nothing of their antics because the lads managed to keep it quiet.

When I finished playing, Emma and I went to Guernsey, and we ended up staying in exactly the same hotel. I remember walking in and seeing that same guy who had worked there in 1997. He looked at me in terror and said, 'Oh no, the others aren't with you are they?' He was pretty relieved that it was just me, and he remembered me as the well-behaved one. Not that I wasn't disorganised; we got there on Friday, and I got a message telling me to remember about my commitments on Saturday. It turned out that I'd forgotten that I was supposed to be having a load of penalties taken at me by a group of kids in Swansea at 9am on Saturday morning. We had no car because we'd flown in. I asked the hotel manager if there was a way of getting the ferry and hiring a car on the other side, and he just handed Emma and me the keys to his car. We caught the evening ferry and drove through the night to Swansea, then drove back to return his car and continue our holiday. I'll never forget that kindness. I guess I was lucky that I was the quiet one in that team!

The problem with the drinking culture was that everyone was also left standing on their own two feet and left to their own devices without a support network in place that challenged the practice. There was nobody in the club questioning their decisions or trying to change them or asking if it was healthy, because they were probably doing the same thing themselves. The manager's door was always open, but if you went to see him then he would probably offer you a glass of wine and you'd be in there all afternoon anyway. So people just didn't talk or open up. They just coped – or maybe thought they were coping.

People talk a lot now about the drinking culture, but it does need to be put into some context. I know the game has changed a lot in the last thirty years in terms of intensity, but we had nowhere near the same levels of physiotherapy and medical treatment, people didn't eat the right things, we had a squad of fourteen outfield players and we played fifty matches a season most seasons without as many muscle injuries as nowadays.

But it could be quite comical – as the trip to Guernsey showed. There were also the times when we went away with Wales – I didn't see the lads for the first couple of days, apart from maybe at breakfast when they were coming back in.

They might have golf days or go to the horse racing and then go out at night. For the first couple of days, I might go down to Cardiff to train. After the game, they all went to Jackson's nightclub in Cardiff, which we used to call the Time Machine because you went in when it was dark and came out when it was light. I went once and thought it was crap, but they had a good time. We'd train on the Sunday and the players would be absolutely abysmal, falling over on the pitch and all sorts. Then on the Monday morning and Tuesday they'd train pretty well and would be ready for the match on the Wednesday.

It all came down to the management with Wales thinking that the morale of the team was incredibly important. That led them to basically giving the players complete licence to have a good time – they believed that it kept the camaraderie within the squad as tight as it could be.

More generally, I look at what it was like then and now, and I do think we're talking about two extremes, with problems in both approaches. Footballers are put in straitjackets nowadays, because they can't do anything. The almost universal use of smartphones means no one can escape scrutiny. There's absolutely nothing wrong with a footballer, or a few footballers, going out and occasionally enjoying themselves, within reason, as it can help teammates bond after a defeat. But you know exactly what the headlines would be in the media, trying to rile the supporters: 'Players out partying hours after defeat', with accompanying images. And that's simply not fair.

It wasn't just about booze. That was simply the means by which they socialised. Clearly footballers now shouldn't drink as much as they used to, but they shouldn't lose the human side that bonded them together. Football, like everything else, has to be about life balance. They must be able to have fun, or we're back to talking about the academy kids who are sheltered from life and so less able to solve problems.

Looking back, I probably worked too hard and so I got the balance wrong just as much as any of the drinkers. I went too far the other way, obsessing about preparation and forgetting the importance of sometimes letting myself go. But I'm still not sure we have that balance right.

You can see why players have detached themselves from fans, because they're scared of criticism and abuse. Combine that with the money the players get, and this enables them to escape from supporters into their huge houses and go to the other side of the world on holiday. And then on top of all that, the clubs believe their players are such valuable assets that they wrap them up in cotton wool to try to protect them. It's all a shame, because it splits up a relationship that used to be much closer. The players used to talk with the fans when they went out on the town. It gave them both a bonding experience that's now gone.

There's also a knock-on effect that comes with castigating footballers for drinking – they now just do it behind closed doors. You hear people within the game talking, and they believe that issues with alcohol are still rife. The only difference is that players in my day were very open about it. Now they can't afford to be seen partying, but perhaps that just changes the environment in which the problem takes place. And drinking alone, or drinking to cope, can be potentially a far more serious problem than drinking heavily in a social context.

Home drinking creates a situation in which modern players are only able to admit the damaging nature of their relationship with alcohol when it's too late. Maybe they wait until they're retired, because if they go public before then they risk losing their place in the team or being released and then left without a club. Maybe they live in fear of being 'found out', hiding their addiction because they are ashamed of it. Both these situations will only make coping with the problem that much harder.

Alcohol

by Anne-Marie Silbiger

Alcohol began its liquid therapy
Holding me close
Too close
Until I could barely breathe

12

SOCIAL MEDIA

'Twitter makes you love people you've never met.
Facebook makes you hate people you actually know.'
Scotty Rosenberg, screenwriter

I didn't set up my Twitter account. I met a guy called Mark, who knew about football and social media in the early days. He was a lovely guy, and he had an idea that we could work together.

At the time, a lot of people would try to contact me to get some advice, most of it for free. I hated it when people managed to get my home address and wrote to me there, sending me DVDs of goalkeepers or letters proposing business ideas they had. It felt like an invasion of privacy, and I have no idea how they managed to get the information. You shouldn't do that to people; it's not on – my home is my sanctuary. I have to keep certain things at arm's length and there has to be a line in the sand, or I'll end up breaking myself and it will consume me whole.

Mark's idea was to create a service where people could talk to me on the phone or via Skype, and get advice on goalkeeper coaching or technique. They could pay and have an hour with me, during which we'd discuss various aspects of their game. We'd have Twitter, Skype and Facebook, and he'd set up the accounts to advertise through that. But it didn't ever really go anywhere.

Mark moved out to Morocco, and I was left with the Twitter account. I've never liked Facebook. I see it as a family thing, a way of people sharing photos of their relatives. But I've always been a private man, and I'd never had any interest in sharing my family life with people I didn't know. I'm not interested in anyone knowing any of that. But I did like Twitter because of its accessibility. If you wonder about something, and you want to reach out and learn about it or go and see someone, that's very hard to do during the working week. But on Twitter you have genuine experts on every topic, right there at your fingertips. As someone who grew up in a small town with a small-town vision, that's extraordinary.

I didn't use it much early on, but then I started to tweet to tell people how I felt. I wasn't necessarily sharing the deepest parts of my personality, just little things that were on my mind. The principal aim was to let people know that I was Neville Southall, not just ex-Everton and Wales goalkeeper Neville Southall. So I had to get across who I was as a person. I wasn't going to be just spouting opinions about goalkeepers in the Premier League. I wanted to convey my thoughts, and then people could either choose to listen to me and follow me, or not.

Nowadays I'll sometimes be deliberately silly, just to see the effect it has. I'm fascinated by the impact a few meaningless words can have on people. I'll tweet something like, 'Seen a badger once in a club in Soho; never went there again,' for no reason other than because I think it's funny. It just is, and people respond with deliberately terrible jokes. You can say what you like if it isn't harmful.

I can put a picture of a kitten on Twitter, and that can be more effective than anything. If people have had a bad day or a bad night and they feel lonely, they might look on Twitter, not like much of what they see, but then see that kitten and feel just a little bit better. They might see it and think, 'That's for me, that is; somebody must be thinking about me.'

I put a hedgehog on the other morning, and someone responded saying, 'Oh God, I really needed that.' What makes that hedgehog so special to that woman? Because it's a nice cute picture, because she needed a lift at that moment, because it made her smile. Sometimes you can keep all your drugs and all your psychiatrists, because at a particular moment and for a particular person, that little hedgehog helped.

That's the simplest thing I can do, but even if only forty people see it and one of them needed it to feel better, it was worth it. How long did it take, twenty seconds? But I've had hundreds of replies from people saying that it cheered them up, and people asking for different animals next time!

I also started a series of tweets about skeletons, where I spoke out against social injustice through the medium of two skeletons. I wanted to choose something that everybody could picture in their mind, but also something that was almost comical. By bringing in an element of comedy, you can make people listen inadvertently to serious points on serious issues. It says things without coming across as preachy. Anyway, that seemed to really connect with people.

It's amazing how tiny things can help change someone's view of a horrible situation. There are people who come close to taking their own lives, but something happens that triggers a positive thought – and that keeps them going. One of the myths about suicide is that these people want to die. It doesn't always work like that. They just don't know how they can carry on coping with the darkness. It's about trying to introduce light into that darkness.

The simplest things you can do are often the most effective, but also the things we forget about most. I'll tweet, telling everyone that I'm thinking about them and that I hope they're all OK, and it will provoke messages from people telling me that they aren't OK. People can say thank you, and I can reply. It starts a conversation, and some of those people might not have had a conversation all day that they've enjoyed. You've given them a link to engage in a positive way. You should never underestimate the power of 'Good morning' and 'Good night'. It means that someone has said it to you and that they're thinking of you. You'll be amazed what a difference that can make to people.

Doing something will always be better than doing nothing. I've had people who haven't responded to me. I've sent them messages checking that they're all right and they haven't come back to me. But then I don't mind that and I certainly don't let it get me down, because they can always look at it later. And it might reassure them then. I know that there are people I speak to on Twitter for whom there will be a time when I stop being of any use to them. Sometimes they move on because they feel better and no longer need to talk to someone. Sometimes they move on because they're getting help elsewhere. That's the reality of the situation; people come and go.

But I love that. It shows that I've succeeded along the way, and those little things are important for me, because it illustrates that you can get things right and that you're not just fighting the tide. And they can pop back in whenever they like. I still check in on their timelines occasionally, just to check that they're getting on OK. But they've moved on, and that's fine.

There's clearly a parental aspect to that, when I think about it. The way they rely on me and then fly the nest because they no longer need that support is like children growing up. The way they can pop back in whenever they like is like grown-up children coming home if they need some more support because something has happened in their personal life. But it also gives me a great buzz, like a proud dad. I stop being so important to them because they've found the strength to move on, and there are always more people I can speak to and help. That's a very heart-warming part of what I do.

It's an amazing feeling to think that you can influence someone's life, even in a very small way, with a few taps of your fingers. And if it does feel good, embrace that enjoyment. Nobody should apologise for helping people making themselves feel all right.

The other thing I began to use Twitter for was to educate myself on certain topics, and to then keep an eye on those topics. Mental health is the obvious one. And through that, I began talking to people who were in need or who just wanted someone to talk to. I do that almost every day.

Sometimes it does get hard. If someone was tweeting me now, that's them as an individual. But they might not know that I'm already dealing with twenty or thirty people at exactly the same time, because they can't see my direct messages. I can completely understand why they feel that they need all of my attention, and it's great that they've reached out, but it does get tiring and it can push you to your limits. I might have someone that starts talking to me at 9pm, and we're still going at 11pm. But it's not fair to say to them, 'Sorry, got to go because I'm busy' because that doesn't help them.

Over the last year I've worked with Unison, the public service trade union, as an international officer, so I'll lean on their calendar to raise awareness of certain topics. One month it might be Black History Month, or Fairtrade issues. Doing this enables me to educate myself on things happening around the world. That's not just escaping my own bubble, but the continent I live in too.

You have footballers and other celebrities that use Twitter, but they employ people to do it for them. That annoys me. Why can't you just do it yourself if you feel it's important to have an account? All they do is retweet corporate shite. I like the people who I can tweet and they will retweet it without even knowing me. During National Suicide Prevention Week, Kym Marsh retweeted some of the stuff. She's got nearly 800,000 followers and there won't be much crossover with me. That will genuinely make a difference. Now I don't know her, but she used her following to do good.

You speak to some people, and they say that their agent won't let them retweet things. It's all managed outside of their control. But that just makes me want to tell them to fuck off. You have a chance to show people who you are, show them that you care. And you won't do it.

Educating myself and then tweeting about those subjects gave me the idea to make my Twitter account a community, where people could know that, at a specific time each week, someone would be raising awareness of a particular issue. So on Monday, Wednesday and Friday (and any other day if they're free), they can take over the account for two hours and have a stage to discuss important issues.

The Twitter takeovers, selfishly, are good for me because they create time for me to get a break. Of course I'm always there, because that's how life works. I sit down on a Saturday and I'm ready to do nothing, and then you get a message asking you to speak to someone because they're struggling. The person might be an Evertonian and they're going through a bad time, so no question, I have to answer that.

But the principle of the takeovers is simple. What's the point of me using the account to talk about trans issues? What am I going to say? 'Oh, I know a few people and they tell me this and that'? I consider myself more educated on these issues than I was before, but I'm not an expert and I haven't gone through those experiences myself. So rather than me just talking about things I've learnt, it made complete sense to temporarily give the account to someone who really knows about them. The good thing is that, by undergoing this process, if I want to say something on an issue or educate myself further, I've got plenty of good contacts close to me that I can speak to and talk to about it first. It makes my own education easier too.

There have been missteps along the way. I had one guy who used it, and he ended up getting into a fight with Alan Sugar. He replied to Sugar about something and, because Sugar assumed it was me on the account, he came back at me and called me an old has-been footballer. I replied to tell him that it wasn't me, but he just said that if it was my account I was responsible for all the content.

I also end up following all sorts of accounts that I know nothing about, because whoever has been on there has followed them for me. But it's all well-meaning. Now when I have takeovers I tell them not to follow people, and to be careful when replying to people. They have a responsibility when using that account, as it does sometimes lead to difficulties. But to actually get messages out there, it has to happen. To do it properly, you have to have spokespeople who have lived in that world. The only thing I can offer truly authoritative advice on is football.

One thing I hate is people that come onto social media and spout shite about things that they barely half-know about, so I wanted to avoid that. This way, you get people informing a large following about what really happens. If it's a trans discussion, it might be how they find clothes, how they find make-up and which brands work best. There are so many practical things. I had a conversation with someone about their operation, about having sex afterwards. They are the things people really want to know about, and they also help to take away the fear and the ignorance. That's more powerful than me just tweeting, 'Don't be a twat to people.'

Sometimes people are reluctant to get involved in the takeovers. Perhaps they're worried about using a different account and believe it sends a mixed message. But I'm trying to give them 150,000 extra people who might listen to their campaign, share it or get involved. Their charity might only have a following of 3,000. I can't force anyone to do it, but I'd like to think most see it as an opportunity. All you have to do on there is talk.

There are four reasons why I might invite an organisation or person to take over the account: 1) it might be interesting to me; 2) I didn't know anything about it and felt I should; 3) it's a small charity that I think deserves more awareness; and 4) it's something that I firmly believe in. For example, we had an HIV charity based in Nevada that funds vending machines that supply clean needles. You sign up with the local government, get a card and then within twenty miles of Las Vegas they'll deliver for free. They do an awful lot of good, and that's something that could work in the UK. Of course, you get people accusing you of saying that it's fine for children to play with needles, but that's nonsense. There's something remarkable about social media that makes people want to disagree with everything and get angry about it.

In the main, the response to the takeovers has been great, but there are obviously exceptions. I was having people from America telling me that I had no idea about certain topics just because they wanted to get a rise. I got to the stage where this sort of thing was getting on my nerves, but I don't let abuse affect me now and you can actually have some fun with it. I suppose that's the whole point of trolls on there – to try to annoy you and get under your skin. But if you manage not to let it bother you, then you remove their oxygen and their power. When you realise that getting annoyed is them winning, you let it wash over you.

Some of my Twitter takeovers gave a voice to the struggles of the transgender community. That did cause a slightly negative reaction initially, but it quickly tailed off. I honestly have faith that most people don't care. Some people might send a message telling me I'm a knob or a weirdo for giving them a voice. And if they do, I can either retweet it and they get slaughtered by other people, or I can just block them. It depends what sort of mood I'm in.

I also think what I am makes a difference. It's fair to say that my type – white, male, late middle-aged, with a professional life in football – was exactly the sort of person that the transgender community might be most fearful of. So if it does send a message that I've welcomed them, that's brilliant. When I was young, we never really understood the concept of gay where I lived, and nobody even mentioned lesbians or bisexuals. I did start to hear the word 'queer' when I was at Everton, but I just hadn't been educated. Instead of turning away from something I didn't understand, I thought it was more appropriate to take a step back, educate myself and ask people about it.

The transphobia is just bizarre. I've had people say to me, 'Well, would you let your daughter go into the same toilets as a trans woman?' 'Yes! What do you think is going to happen? And why are you judging them like that?' These people are obsessed with toilets! There's almost no point continuing with a conversation like that, because they just don't want to listen. It reflects far worse on them than on the person they're attacking, but they just don't see it.

There's a certain age group, a certain block of people, who you can imagine have just remained close-minded and never seen anything outside of their bubbles in their entire lives. But it does make you wonder whether they feel guilty about something they've done in their past. Because there's a generation for whom bottling things up until they started to fester became the norm. I think that religion probably played a part in that, but so did the media. It isn't that long since newspapers treated homosexuality as if it were a disease, or at least a flaw in someone's psyche. If you had a gay person on TV, they made them so out there and camp that it became a parody. But what is a gay person? There is no stereotype. They're just people who feel differently to you.

I speak to a guy who dresses up in women's clothes, but who exactly is he offending? Yet some middle-aged individuals think that cross-dressers are going to attack people. I honestly don't know what they've been told or read, and why they haven't questioned it. As I've already mentioned, I guarantee that if someone had come out in our Everton dressing room, every single player would have backed them. We'd have told them that we were fully behind them, and fuck everyone else. Because they're just normal blokes. There's going to be homophobic people, but we've got to stop pandering to them and stop giving airtime to their unacceptable views.

I honestly believe that in twenty years' time, if we're able to remove the politics of hatred in this country, then the population will become more open and tolerant. But people have got to have conversations about it. I like what I like, you like what you like, and neither of us need be offended about each other. We can both lead the lives that we want to live without interference, without judgement and without hatred.

Social media is brilliant for its ability to force collective action. People come on and I honestly believe that they can drive things through. You won't get to everyone, and you might not force wholesale change, but you can make a difference. We had the stem cell people come on, and they were asking people to try to become potential donors. That night, they received far more offers than they normally would, but even if it only gets one extra donor, what has it cost? Nothing. That night opened them up to a new audience, and it made a tangible difference.

I think people in general have underestimated social media, and its ability to be used for genuine good and to enable all of us to take definitive action. Now it might not be in any psychotherapy textbook, but I'm confident that I'm using it as best I can to help people. Look at it like this: how else can you get through to ten million people in five minutes? There's no other way. But tweet the right people or get retweeted by them, and you can. You can hit such an extraordinary number of people just by spending two minutes typing something. Forget all the letters you'd needed to have posted thirty years ago or the phone calls you'd have had to have made. Frank Bruno retweeted some posts on mental health issues – there's 120,000 followers. Jamie Carragher is as good as gold – and he's got 1.4 million. If they share stuff, people get to see it and they genuinely listen. It makes a difference.

We had Labour MP John Ashworth, who came on to answer questions, and I think he did really well. I said to him that it would be good for him because that's what politicians are supposed to do: engage with the public in a normal way on a medium people know. And I think it changes how he's perceived, because he doesn't know what's coming, unlike with scripted interviews and speeches. He could have had people giving him all manner of abuse or have people asking what he's doing for the cleaners in their local hospital because he's the shadow health secretary. In that way, coming on Twitter isn't just a tool for communication but a chance for you to show a part of yourself to people. To be able to do that makes you a good politician.

I think that people in this country feel that they're powerless to actually challenge politicians and get them to care about what matters to them, and making more of an effort to communicate is one way of helping to address that suspicion. It's also the hardest way, but it helps persuade people that you haven't just got your own agenda at heart. I was chuffed when Ashworth came on, because it proves that someone in his position can do it.

I have a vision of other people agreeing to pass over their Twitter accounts for takeovers to raise awareness of certain issues. It doesn't even have to be people with huge followings, just those committed to helping. They could use social media in the absolute best way, by giving those in need of a stage or a platform exactly that.

But this hasn't happened yet, for whatever reason. I think everyone just closes up and increasingly thinks inside their own box. Everyone lives so fast and is only concerned with their own lives. When you wake up in the morning, what do you think about? Yourself. Your family, your friends, your work. Everything else is a bonus. I think people have plans to do things, to push themselves to do more, but time goes too quickly for them. Suddenly a week, a month, a year has passed and all you've done is move further into your own bubble. People tell themselves that they can't do something now because it isn't the right time. But it's never the right time.

Add to that the fact that people tend to concentrate more on the things that make them money in a materialistic society. If they're meant to finish at 5pm, are they prepared to stay an extra thirty minutes to get something else done or do they think, 'No, I want to get out. I'm not paid for that.'

I completely understand that attitude, but it does threaten to increase the 'us against them' mentality that's growing and growing, and which damages society. I get that everyone feels that they can't be bothered because they're tired and they just want to have more time for themselves, but there has to be a bit more joined-up thinking. And there has to be a desire to prioritise what really matters to make things better, even if it's hard and you might not get paid for it.

I think you can see it in football too. There's far more individualism – in terms of their ambition – among players. The game's increasingly become about having a successful career and making money, rather than winning as a team and earning glory for the club and the city. Players now sign for clubs that have no hope of winning major trophies purely for the money, and that certainly didn't happen when I played.

Which brings me back to social media and being a player. My initial thought was that I wouldn't have used social media as a player, but then I wonder whether I might have done so because I had things to say. It's very difficult thing to know when you were brought up without the technology being available to you. You have to remember that the first mobile phone I ever owned was attached by a lead in my Volvo, and it was bloody massive. Even when I had that phone, I had mixed feelings about the way it kept me constantly connected. I went through a period when, no matter where I'd been playing, I used to get these calls as soon as I got into the car after a night match from someone I didn't know. All they'd do was stay silent but remain on the line. At first I used to turn it off, but eventually I thought that I'd have a bit of fun. So I let them call, answered it and just started talking to them. I'd talk them through bits of the journey, or say that the sky was lovely or tell them about my saves. Eventually I upped the ante by whistling really loudly to try to annoy them. On reflection, that might have been when they stopped calling. You can potentially multiply how annoying that was by ten times on social media. If a high-profile player is running their own account then they must expect a lot of abuse – and that can't be healthy. So they get someone to run it for them, and then there's no point to it anyway.

But I do believe that the vast increase in the money available in the game today, compared with the amount the average person or family gets, creates an additional moral duty for players to help others, because it also confers a far greater power to change lives. These people have the power, status and wealth to be true leaders by example.

But for the clubs it goes beyond moral duty and becomes sound business sense too. If Everton help out someone in need, someone who has reached their lowest ebb and is given a leg up, is that person ever going to say anything bad about Everton again? Or are they likely to feel much closer to the club? That person could have a business, or know someone that does, who might take on a sponsorship deal or buy into the corporate hospitality. That might be an extreme example, but you see the point; helping other people looks good, especially when it's done off your own back. It's an easy PR victory.

Now you can't set that aside from the moral duty. As pillars of the community, with vast revenues and hopefully a reliance on producing local players, clubs should be falling over themselves to be providers for their local areas. But then you could say the same about individual people too. I wish more people would look outside of their own lives, realise that there are those far less fortunate than themselves and understand their own power to help. Social media is potentially the most powerful tool in social care, and yet we've allowed it to become warped by our own self-interest. We must recapture it and maintain it as a tool for good.

Social media

by Anne-Marie Silbiger

Be kind they said
but only for a day or two
Hold your ire they said
but only for a day or two

13

HELPING OTHERS

*'Children need us to help them find their way in life
and cope with losing it, not to give them a label.'*
Kay Brophy, psychologist and family practitioner,
the Acorn family

One of the unifying themes of this book is that everyone has
to go through some shit. Some go through worse experiences
than others, but it usually comes down to whether people are
able to find a way of getting through it and find the help they
need to make life easier. Some can. But some can't – and,
hopefully, that's where I come in.

The problem comes when people become blinkered.
Everybody lives in their own bubble, and they find it increasingly hard to exist outside of it. Now the whole idea is to take
yourself out of that bubble and ask people, 'How are you
doing? What have you got on? What do you need?' And then
you hope people will do the same for you if you need it.
Whether that actually happens, and whether anyone actually
meets you halfway, is the biggest issue in society.

The more money an organisation has, the more it tends to
close itself off from other organisations, ones that could be
mutually beneficial. And football is like that too. I spoke to a

manager once and I asked him why he was using a particular goalkeeping coach when he was virtually useless. The answer I got was that the manager knew the goalkeeping coach had his back, and to him that was the most important thing. That goalkeeping coach would end up dragging this particular manager down, because you're only as good as your coaches. How is he that insecure that he's prepared to depend on someone because he knows he'll agree with him? People are obsessed with self-preservation.

Although I was very focused on being the best that I could be, I was already helping other people in my clubs. I'd try and help the apprentice goalkeepers as much as I could and check in to see if they needed anything. Some players might have been more protective of their position, but that wasn't in me. At the end of the day we're all eventually going to get replaced and there's nothing you can do to stop that other than being the best you can be. So you're far better off helping others be the best they can be too. That was taught to me by the senior goalkeepers I worked with when I was younger, who were always brilliant with me.

I speak to people with depression and anxiety now, and I try to work out what I and they can do individually, and how we can do it together. Maybe they just needed the right person to come along with the right idea to help them. They might have to try twenty people or they might have to try one, but it's all about giving them the opportunity to try as many as it takes. Let's say that they can't get out of bed because they feel too anxious; we can work on that together. Tomorrow, let's try to get out of bed and then get back into bed, and celebrate that they achieved it. Then the next day get out of bed and try to stay out a little longer, and celebrate that too. Then go downstairs and come back. And try to visualise getting out of bed and staying out of bed, try to imagine it being OK.

I also get them to keep a diary of how far they've come and remind them to read through that diary to feel good about the journey to date. That can often help them during the darker times when they feel that they can't get out of bed, because they've already proved that they can do it.

If someone talks to me who's having dark thoughts, I tell them anything I think they need to hear to get them back. You have to get them to a point where you can get through to them more easily, and that requires them to be open. If they ask further down the line why I said what I said, I'll be honest and say that everything I told them was because I care about them and wanted them to come closer to me from that meta-phorical edge.

All I try to do is to be as positive as I can be and encourage them to talk. Then I can pick up on anything they say, because that will give me clues. It's very hard if it happens on Twitter, because if they just send me a message there isn't an awful lot to go on – and you can read things two or three different ways. But I'll go on their social media profile, and look for a hook on there that gives me something to try to talk to them about.

It's amazing what they'll tell me, because they tell me everything. It really opens your eyes. They often work on the principle that it's better out than in, and that's absolutely right. Of course, sometimes they think they have told me too much and they block me. But you can't dwell on what you did to deserve that – simply continue to be open and help the next person.

I have to say now that I do it because I want to, not because I consider that I'm doing some amazing feat or going on some worthy campaign. I can do it, it's easier to do it than ever before because of Twitter and I want to do it. And I've had help from people, so I'm trying to pay that forward. Or maybe I'm just a nosey bastard! I guess that depends which way you look at it.

For me it's about linking people up. One of the things I like about the Twitter takeovers I run is that they often lead them to someone else who's prepared to help. I did something at a mental health hospital in Newport, where they desperately needed materials to improve the buildings, and some of the saws they were having to use to make improvements looked like they came from Victorian times. I alerted people on Twitter to get the word out there, and some guy drove a band saw down from the Midlands to give it to them.

There are some brilliant people out there, but they just need to be connected to each other. And if all I have to do is say, 'You go with them and you can help them,' then great. All I've done is connected a helper with someone that needs help.

But I also had that support from other people. Everywhere I've been and asked for help, people have either said that they'd help me or introduced me to someone who could. When I first went to the school I work in now, all I needed was the help of Evertonians. After I asked for help, they rushed in. That's incredibly special, and I'll never forget it. So all that hard work on the training ground to be the best I could be for the club paid off way down the line.

The thing about using social media in this way is that you realise just how many people are there to help, an almost frightening number. There are millions. But here's the thing – if I'm doing what I can, and other people do the same, all those people can be helped. We have a tool to connect people.

I had someone whose girlfriend had taken their own life, there was nowhere they wanted to go and get help, and they just needed to talk to someone. You can't help everyone, but if you can help someone you help them, and if you can't you don't. And there's a long, long list of those who you can help.

Of course, I've also made mistakes. I remember coming out of work one day and seeing one of the temps – I asked him quickly if he was all right, as you often do on autopilot in passing. He went, 'No, not really,' and I just said, 'OK, mate, see you later. Keep well.' As I drove home I realised that I should have stopped to talk to him further. I was on the way to pick the kids up and running a little late, but I got that wrong.

It forever amazes me how people cope. They hold down regular jobs while dealing with mental health problems, and they still manage to do what they need to do. It's truly extraordinary and takes unthinkable courage. It's hard for people who've never gone through such debilitating experiences to really understand. Mental health issues aren't something that can be switched off like a tap; they haunt you, day in, day out. Even when you feel well, they lurk somewhere inside you, waiting to reveal themselves and knock you off your feet.

Surely we have a responsibility to ensure that the system takes care of people with these problems, not just processes them. But we don't. And the system only reacts, and too rarely proactively addresses the causes that lead people into these places of mental struggle. At the very least, we owe them a plan, a way of moving forward from the moment they struggle to try to improve things. But again, we don't. We merely react to each stage on the road downhill.

With the right solution, I think most people can get through most things. But sometimes even the solutions aren't available. If one of our kids suffers a family tragedy, where's he going to go? What happens now? If he has no relationship with his parents and is struggling at school, what's going to happen to him?

If you ask any school what they want to concentrate on, first and foremost it should be the well-being of the children. How can you be concentrating in maths if you have so much other shit going on in your life? How can you reach your full potential as a child if we can't help you in your life outside the classroom? Kids get to primary level and they have problems. They move on to secondary level and they have problems. They leave school and they still have problems, and then they're thrown into the mess of the real world and have to face those problems without a support network. Why not try to sort it out earlier on?

The problem is that these aspects of a child's education – their mental health and well-being – are almost impossible to assess. How do you measure what I do on Twitter, talking to people? You can't. It's just stuff that happens and hopefully makes a difference. But that difference isn't quantifiable, and so it can't be ranked.

Schools are the same. How do you measure the success of a kid that comes to us with a whole host of issues, continually struggles in a classroom environment but at the end of it gets into an apprentice scheme that they love and are genuinely good at? Now to them, their apprenticeship is far more applicable to the real world than doing well at science. But the system might consider them a failure. There's one set of rankings that people care about – academic achievement – and that ranking system has been deemed the be-all and end-all. So you can see why schools are ruled by it.

But the reality is that there simply isn't enough funding for kids who struggle, and that's partly because the system is set up badly. Again it goes back to setting proaction over and above reaction. Children can be sent all over the country. They get excluded or it's recommended that they leave mainstream education, and they might come to our school. We do all we can, but sometimes we cannot adequately deal with their needs or problems using our resources. We offer them as many things as we can, but now and then we reach the end of what we can do.

These kids are taken far away from their home, where they might actually have a small support network, and they're sent somewhere they don't want to be, they don't know anyone and they're powerless to choose. They're already in a mental state where they don't fit in, and it's made been five times worse. How would someone even without such problems cope? But these kids become guinea pigs in a struggling system. Now, if we helped them at the start of the cycle, maybe that money could be saved. And, more importantly, maybe they could be helped better before things got too much. We are a reactive society, and nobody suffers more from this than kids with learning and behavioural difficulties.

Some of our kids go through full-on crises. Life is fucking tough. They might come in in the morning and they haven't slept, or have had patchy sleep for a few hours. They come in and all they want to do is sleep. We have a therapy room, so do we let them use it to catch up on sleep or do we shove double maths or science in their faces? If they need sleep, they need sleep. But there's a battle at the heart of the education system there. You can't just throw a blanket over everyone and expect them to fit under it successfully. It goes back to the problem with tunnel vision, focusing on the end goal without realising what might actually matter on the journey to reach it.

For us, it's about an individual approach to every kid. But in mainstream education, where you have thirty in a class and each teacher might see a hundred and fifty different children a day, it's very hard to maintain that individual approach. It's like having forty players in a first-team squad and trying to implement a philosophy. You get cliques and factions, and it's almost impossible to do anything other than react to the issues that arise because of them.

One of the fashionable approaches at the moment with anxiety is talking – let's talk, let's talk. Now I understand the good intention of that message, but what does it actually mean? Let's talk. To whom? When? What happens if I'm alone? That message risks accidentally placing the onus on the sufferer. Some of the people I talk to are truly alone. They can't think straight. I've had people convinced that the doctors want to kill them, so they can't afford to go to sleep. 'Let's talk' doesn't always help them.

The solution is to know where you're going to point them next. Thankfully, I've got help from people that have worked with the Samaritans, so I can say honestly to them, 'I don't know what to do at this point or what I should be advising,' while, crucially, giving them the next point of contact, someone who will understand their situation the best they can without having spoken to them. Again, it's about knowing what you don't know and where your limitations lie.

I'm constantly learning. Some people I can't work out, some people I can, but there are failures. There will be people where I can't see where they're coming from or where they're going. That's the reality. But I'm a strong believer that there's a motivator out there for everyone, a person that can connect with another particular person. You just have to find the right one.

My grand vision for helping others is campaigning for a vast improvement in the willingness to work together. We have the NHS and a load of charities that work alongside each other, so what are we doing with them? If those hundreds of mental health charities got together, went to the government and said that they were going to strike if funding for services didn't improve, there would be a crisis. They would be heard.

I said at a suicide awareness conference that if someone goes to A&E with dark thoughts, they're likely to be told to sit somewhere for two hours until someone can see them. But if there was a long list of charities approved by the NHS, someone could pick this person up and work with them. The charities could be regulated, have their own council, and go to the government and demand change together.

We also need to vastly improve the reach of mental health charities. Why is there not a simple app for phones with a list for every hospital catchment that could help you? The NHS could then approach people who are current and relevant to the younger generation who would be ambassadors for the app. Who doesn't want that? Who doesn't want to help save the NHS? Who wants to break it up, other than those who have a vested financial interest in doing so? So you get those ambassadors to tweet or use Facebook to signpost the information to young people, and they will follow it.

What does all this cost in the great scheme of things? You save money on the advertising that so few young people and vulnerable people see, and save money in the long run anyway by being so proactive. It's a far more effective way of getting to the people in this country who really need help, and a cost-effective way too. If all of Everton's players did it semi-regularly, and you got Wayne Rooney into the mix too, you could probably reach ten million people very easily – and that's before it got shared and became well known. And they don't really need to be that active on Twitter, just tweeting and retweeting the odd thing.

I talked to an Assembly Member (AM) in Wales. We've got universities in Cardiff, Swansea, Bangor, Aberystwyth and Wrexham. I asked him why we couldn't have a mental health radio station, and make sure it runs through the night. It would cost a few quid, but you could get experts on an evening to come on and talk about a particular subject – and many would volunteer. The Samaritans would occasionally take over, and trainee counsellors could come in, take part in a talk show and improve their own learning.

Not long after, I spoke to a number of other AMs and asked why, when you buy a phone in this country, it doesn't automatically have the Samaritans app loaded onto it. You could trial it in a particular city if that was deemed appropriate. Then people wouldn't have to search out the number – and at the time when they really need it, you risk them not doing so. After all, if you're struggling that much, do you go online and search for the number? But the moment that they've clicked on and engaged with that app, they've shown strength in reaching out. There's simple things you can do.

Finally, I've spoken to AMs about getting all the Labour candidates in Wales to create a ring of mental health. So once a week, say a Sunday night when vulnerable people can often feel most alone, they give their Twitter account over to a different mental health charity and we would pick a particular topic. There's people out there who want to help with this. They don't want to get paid, but would do it to raise awareness because they're good people.

I've got lots of ideas, but they all come down to reaching as many vulnerable people as you can and making it as simple as possible for them to connect with an organisation or other people. Because simply taking a step, however small, is a start. It's no good creating an initiative with a few posters, and then just sitting back and assuming you've done your bit. That can quickly turn into a box-ticking exercise.

Everton have two million followers on Twitter. If you got 100,000 of those fans to pledge £1 a week (and I know not all can), you'd have over £5 million a year, just like that. Imagine the difference you could make in Liverpool. You could start by putting the money into mental health initiatives, or into stocking food banks. Or you could say that people who volunteer at food banks for at least ten hours per week have their council tax paid, thereby creating a system of incentivised charity. It's not a lot of money to football, but it is to the vulnerable. Everton could double the amount per week that was pledged, making a massive difference and doing so much good. Bring some more mental health charities under your wing and become a truly transformative club on societal issues.

They could become a leader for a movement. What happens if Manchester United do it? What if Everton go to Anfield, to Liverpool, and say that we need to do this jointly, as a city? You have twice the power, but also display incredible unity. Before you know it, fans are rushing to represent their club. If it goes back into the community, people will help.

What if they invested the money so that every kid under sixteen could be guaranteed a certain amount of free football coaching? Before you know it, more kids are playing football and enjoying something. What if every club does it, and it becomes a football movement? It would help to reconnect the clubs and the game with their local communities, something that so many supporters have sadly lost.

I do think that football clubs in general are brilliant. Everton in the Community are a wonderful organisation, looking at different ways to make a difference. But if you get that £100,000 a week and get literal buy-in from the club, then you're not scratching around for funding. Everton had £190 million in revenue at the last count. They can do this. And they should, too. Never underestimate the power of a football club – financially and culturally – to make lives better for others.

* * *

The need to create support networks only became more apparent during the coronavirus crisis. I do think that a lot more people tried to help others during this miserable period, which was a great thing. Some of the people I've worked with on Twitter came to the fore again and pushed information out to try to reach the most vulnerable.

But let's be clear: this wasn't government help, it was people helping people. It was people doing things off their own backs because their moral alarm had sounded and they realised that there were others in need. That's absolutely brilliant. I went on Twitter every day, and you'd see people running competitions or putting on quizzes or doing little shows to keep people entertained. Amid the tidal wave of shitty news, in places Twitter actually became a place for social interaction once again, rather than just a firestorm of competing opinions.

And then you've got the people you don't see, those who opened up their direct messages for people to chat to them as and when they needed it. There was probably more help being offered than ever before, and that's because it took a crisis to make people realise that they needed to get others through this. I heard from people who said that they had nobody to talk to, so we set up a 'corona club', where for an hour every day they could come on and just chat. I had the Open University on to explain all the courses they do for free to give extra structure to the lives of people who were unable to go to work.

The thing I found hardest personally was trying to concentrate on tasks when there was no end date in sight. It became very easy to put things off until the next day. I did a three-hour course on panic attacks one day, and it took me about seven hours because your mind just wanders without the usual structure of everyday life. I wanted to start as many mini-projects as I could, because I could do a little bit of each every day – that way I was, to an extent, replicating the format of my daily working life and keeping to a routine.

But this crisis must be a wake-up call to people. We have been living our lives at a million miles an hour and we've been killing the planet in pursuit of the capitalist dream. It takes something like this to make people question whether they need to slow down a bit, and concentrate on what and who really matters. They may question their own practices, what they think about the people who run their lives and how they want to change their lives for the better. My dream – and call me an optimist if you like – is that they also realise the importance of helping others to make their lives better too.

Helping others

by Anne-Marie Silbiger

Choose to help others
Be the one who speaks up
Make it a life worth living
Hold out your hand

14

INEQUALITY

'Love is the appropriate response.'
Alan Wright
(@ScrtDrugAddict)

The treatment of vulnerable people in the UK is a national scandal. More than that – it is *the* national scandal of our times. People are getting away with trampling the country into the dirt, but everyone attacks the wrong people. There was a news story I read recently about ambulance and police response times being unacceptable, but people were attacking the emergency services for their efforts. It's insane, absolutely ridiculous.

I believe that as a country we have a duty to sell our children a message of 'Be who you want to be'. But we don't. We tell them that you can't do this and you can't be that. And we have people in charge who actively pursue that agenda. It's a stupid attitude, one that permeates from the top of society right down to the very bottom and which persists because those at the top are very happy to keep those at the bottom where they are. If you want a proper society, get proper people to run it and judge them by how they treat the most vulnerable.

It seems to me that people are so low that they don't know who to turn to for help. You have social workers who have to react to things but can't cope. You have the police who can't always turn up quickly – and it's the same with the other emergency services. You have funding cuts across the board to the services that offer the greatest amount to the most vulnerable. How can it be acceptable to offer less to the worst off?

Nobody seems to have yet said that we've had enough. But it's coming. Giving up won't always be the answer. The trick employed by those in charge is stopping people from realising that they don't have to keep accepting that they're getting pissed on and told that it's raining. Somebody will come from somewhere who will start uniting people, not necessarily even a politician. They will persuade people to get behind him or her, and they will make it known that they've had enough.

If Brexit goes badly, it will get worse. Hopefully, people will realise that they've been lied to. There will be a backlash. The only barriers to this happening at the moment are that they don't realise it yet, and that they don't have, for whatever reason, someone who they consider to be the right figurehead to follow. Jeremy Corbyn got the students and the under-25s on board, but he wasn't able to rally the support of large swathes of the working class. It will take someone exceptional to extricate people out of their tunnel vision.

The worry now is that it's those who are intent on dividing that are coming to the fore more than those who are trying to bring people together. And the support that these divisive individuals get comes from people who are militant in their beliefs, a product of the media and politicians driving people apart.

There's obviously a feeling in this country that we can't get what we want or have as much money as we want because someone is trying to keep us down. And people are taught that this is the fault of outsiders, or of those around them, rather than because society has been deliberately weighted against them. That leads to them becoming more protective of their own interests, so they look after themselves and what they have, and they mistrust everyone else, helping to create a society that has become a series of 'us against them' battles. But it shouldn't be like that. We should be taught to question why one of the biggest economies in the world has such gross inequality. We have eighty years – or more, if we're lucky – and we have to try to make the most of them. But in doing so, you should try to let as many other people as possible make the most of theirs too.

The only way to beat hatred and division is through love and kindness. That's not just a throwaway line, it's very real. We have to learn to look after each other more, rather than allowing ourselves to have our generosity worn down. It's as if people are living with a huge boot grinding them down, keeping them in place. 'Yes, your life is hard, but that's because it's meant to be hard and it will always be hard because that's your lot.' So what's going to happen to the kids coming out of school in three or four years' time, if things get worse economically and socially?

It's no wonder that people suffer from mental health issues when they feel that they have no hope and that there's no escape. To them, it doesn't feel like there's anything positive coming out of anywhere – it's just a constant cycle of bad news and blame. People don't think that they can trust anyone in the media, or in politics. They don't believe that anyone has their back. The support systems are horrendously bad. What does that make people think about themselves?

The whole structure is built upon a series of select lies. That the people at the bottom of society are all lazy and don't want to work. That foreign people are taking all of our jobs. That Europe is to blame for our ills. That the people at the top are looking out for the people at the bottom. You take away all hope from people and you get them to believe these lies, and their lack of hope quickly turns into resentment.

If you're fed all that information when you already have anxiety or depression, it makes it ten times worse. Life becomes a series of 'You can't do that' episodes, which inevitably damages self-esteem. And if you take it so far, it makes people think that there's no point to life. But through love and kindness, we can create hope. With hope comes confidence. With confidence comes power. With power comes action.

This country is full of great people who have been taught not to see what's really going on. But the have-nots will eventually say that enough is enough, and the bigger the gap widens, the angrier people will get. The unions will get behind it and people will move. People have been ground down to nothing over the last decade, and their only choice is to live day by day. Stick a plaster over it today and we'll worry about it tomorrow. That's all the NHS can do. That's all our care services can do. That's all the education system can do. That's all mental health services can do. Because everything is so underfunded.

People at present admire the strength with which an opinion is held more than they value logic and realism. The sheer intensity of the opinion persuades them. They aren't interested in realism because they think that their real life is crap – and they're not happy, so they're content to be sold a pipe dream or an illusion. If Boris Johnson says he'll build a bridge over the Irish Sea, they approve of it. But 'He says what he thinks' isn't enough if you can't do what you say, and what you say makes things worse for the most vulnerable. We have the power, we can make change, yet we're hardwired to think that we're powerless.

But we need to remember this: a society is only working if everybody is looked after. It isn't working if it looks after you and me but not other people. That's just a society skewed towards us; we're simply the lucky ones.

I don't mind if people work hard, pay their taxes and want to keep more of their money. If someone earns £100,000 a year and works a seventy-hour week, I can understand that they feel that they've worked damn hard. That's the same if someone earns £10,000 and wants to keep more too. But the system only works if society is looking after everyone, and right now it's not.

People have become so trapped by their tunnel vision, and that has taught them not to help others. But everyone I meet wants to help others. I think there are two extremes: those who understand the need to help as many other people as they can, and those who will only ever want to take for themselves – and screw the rest. There are the selfless and the selfish.

Then there's a massive group of people who sit somewhere in the middle. They'd consider themselves to be helpful, but for whatever reason have become selective in who they want to help. Now obviously they don't like that accusation, because it challenges them as individuals, so it only makes them more closed off. And it's very hard to persuade them to be better when politics and the media are actively campaigning for them not to change.

One way to lighten the load would be to take more from those at the top. You had the story about Denise Coates, the CEO of Bet365, who took home a £323 million salary in 2019. I just don't see how anyone can work hard enough to justify that wage while others in society remain helpless.

Football comes into this discussion too. One of the reasons for the great disconnect between supporters and players is that you have players earning £200,000 a week for kicking a ball around very well. I fully understand the argument that there's so much money in the sport that they – or their agents – can command those wages. I understand too that plenty of them do their bit with charities, and that's great, but you can see how the disconnect is established and how it has become widened. The top end of society – in terms of wealth – has spiralled out of control, while those at the bottom are struggling.

We're getting to a stage where the top six clubs will always be the top six clubs, and that's just not right. What this does is persuade some of the clubs below them to disconnect with their communities in pursuit of those above. Everton are moving to a new stadium not because the atmosphere will be better, but because commercially they cannot afford to stay where they are because the gap has already been artificially created to make things harder. West Ham? Exactly the same. But that doesn't necessarily make either of these clubs 'better' in the true sense of the word.

If society is on the edge of something hugely significant, I think football is approaching the same point. Perhaps it's already there. The richest clubs are already trying to become their own broadcasters and doing everything themselves in an attempt to keep all the money. So the richest get richer, English football creates a monster that it cannot control – and it never stops. When they become dissatisfied with that, the top clubs will do something else, whether it's a Super League or something else. And we'll effectively end up with a closed shop, like the NFL in the States.

But the coronavirus crisis has changed everything, including people's perception of football and footballers. Football is incredibly important to so many people, but it took a truly global crisis to make people realise that it actually doesn't really matter. All the clubs were having discussions about getting the season finished and finding creative ways to make that happen in order to retain their broadcasting revenues, but there was a large section of society – including plenty of football fans – for whom it became increasingly unimportant. When you're trying to keep safe, when you're worried about your loved ones dying and your partner having to expose themselves to a deadly virus while working in a hospital, it hammers home what truly matters. People are more worried about their health, their jobs, their financial situation and the future of the country than the Premier League being finished.

That's not to say that football isn't important anymore, because obviously it's a huge national pastime and to some it's the defining measure of normality. Going to the match or watching a game in the pub with their mates or on the sofa at home is one of the staples of their social activity, and that's not unimportant. But the pandemic has reinforced the message that health and well-being must come first.

In that context, football has to be careful that it doesn't cross the line and try to make itself the be-all and end-all of everything in a post-coronavirus world. Yes, it will be lovely to have football back on a fully normal programme, but people are going to be far less well-off after the crisis. They might not be able – or willing – to spend £60 on a match ticket. The Premier League has to be prepared to adjust its behaviour accordingly, rather than merrily carrying on as if nothing has happened. Broadcasters will operate on the belief that people have been starved of football and so will be eager to gorge on it again, and to some extent that's true. But I wouldn't be surprised if, over time, it became slightly less popular, particularly going to matches at the highest level given the prices involved. This is a time of necessary financial hardship. In such circumstances, football cannot continue to take the piss out of fans. People will ask why clubs and players deserve quite so much money, while they're all so hard up.

Footballers are paid extortionate amounts of money, but can that carry on? Will there be the money for £100 million transfer fees or players being paid £300,000 a week if the clubs know there's a danger of the pandemic returning and blowing their business model out of the water? As businesses, they will need contingency plans in place from now on. And the owners of some clubs will have lost a lot of money over this period anyway. Perhaps their model no longer works.

I think that can be a good thing. It's time to bring a little more reality into the game and work out what's truly important. We've heard of so many clubs over the last few months that are facing financial ruin because of lost income. Every league below the Premier League is creaking. If football *is* truly our national game, the notion of the football family must be more than just words – if we're all going to stick together as this family, non-league clubs are as important as Premier League clubs. Nobody could have reasonably predicted the pandemic, at least not to the extent of the impact it has had on our lives and on football. But it has laid bare just how many clubs are living hand-to-mouth and have been plunged into trouble. And that has to change.

The saddest thing is that in all the reaction to this, so little was done to help others. That's not to say that clubs didn't do anything, because there were food-bank donations, care lines and community schemes implemented. And individuals did great things, like Gary Neville giving up his hotel to NHS workers; that was a brilliant thing to do. But those clubs and players at the top have access to extraordinary amounts of money in comparison to lower-league clubs. If you're in a family, you look after everyone within it. So where are the bigger clubs saving those below them? Plenty of their players came through that lower-league structure, and they're happy to use the smaller clubs when they want to loan players out.

Take Chelsea. They were on the verge of going out of business before Roman Abramovich took over. They should have an understanding of the financial hardship of the clubs below them now, and empathise with them. They should be prepared to agree to a more equable distribution of broadcasting revenues. So why isn't there an enforced tax on these richest clubs to help out others further down the ladder? This is supposed to be our game, not theirs. There must be a system to protect the traditional league system and the clubs within it. If that means enforced wealth distribution, then so be it. And any big club that flounces off and refuses to do their bit will be on the receiving end of a backlash from supporters. Sometimes it takes a crisis for people to see that things must change. There's a culture of greed that has taken over football, and it's not sustainable.

Enforced wealth distribution in football is one answer – perhaps the only answer – to the problem, but in society as a whole it's a lot more complicated than that. People at the top helping those at the bottom is great, and all power to the ones who do, but they shouldn't have to. It shouldn't work like that. Charities only fill the gaps where organisations and funding have let people down. The government's responsibility should be to find a method for helping those at the bottom without relying upon charitable gestures. The government should be obliged to give more, and there should be legislation to ensure this. They should be investing in a society in which everyone is looked after. Instead, many politicians are invested in a have and have-not society.

The media is hugely responsible for the continuity of this vastly unequal society, and it's horrendous. They are more than complicit – they have led it. The change in tone over the last first years is remarkable, and it's left us with both Donald Trump and our very own version, 'Donald Trump with a thesaurus', as he's been called. Europe is the bad guy. Foreigners are the bad guys. So and so are the bad guys. It's appalling.

The media have such a massive influence now. They parrot half-truths and mistruths from the government, and it should be criminal. They've becomes a massive driver of intolerance, and it shouldn't be that way. I find it absolutely bizarre that people can preach intolerance and feel no shame for it. Boris Johnson has done exactly what Donald Trump has done, which is to deliberately divide people to create political chaos, which he then claims he will address and rebuild the country. Spout your lies as many times as you can – and people start believing them. How do they get away with that?

I think today, more than ever in this country, actually finding the truth is harder than ever. So many things are being said in a way that suits the media's agenda that people have become accustomed to not knowing what to believe. Here's one paper saying this, and here's another saying that. People have been brought up to believe what they read in the tabloids or hear on TV, but they're all saying so many different things, and our lives have become so consumed by the media that people get stuck.

The scary thing is that we now have bigger things to worry about. The planet has had it, and we're going to have to work together, properly together, to help fight that battle. But will we? Or will we keep looking after only ourselves, and in doing so fail to look after anyone properly?

Where I work in Blaenau Gwent, people told me that they were voting to leave the European Union because they had been fed the line that foreigners were taking their jobs. There was an interview on the news where someone said that the EU had done nothing for us, and behind them was the road that had been built with EU money. Now there's comparatively high unemployment in the area, but they've been taught to blame the wrong people. They fear something that doesn't exist, and it's all built on deliberate misinformation.

Social media plays a huge part in people's lives, but there's very little fact-checking around what people are saying. The only response is people calling things out as wrong, but that only becomes a smaller version of two tabloid front pages saying different things. The whole sorry situation causes people to do one of two things: either they become influenced by the people who shout the loudest, those who tend to espouse the most extreme views, or they fall in on themselves, creating their own echo chamber and becoming a belief system of one. They trust nothing and no one.

Those with extreme and divisive opinions succeed because they cultivate a charisma that speaks to people who want to be convinced and have their niggling insecurities played upon. Tell them other people are taking their jobs and they believe it, because it panders to their fear. It doesn't even matter if it's true or not if you can get people to accept it as a fact. And if they do get caught out lying, they just hit back by accusing the naysayers of lying themselves or blustering their way through.

I try to speak the truth on Twitter, but some people just say, 'Oh, it can't be that bad, you're just scaremongering.' But it is that bad – they just have no concept of a reality outside their own. These people would have stood on the deck of *Titanic* and said, 'It's only a scratch, push on to New York.' It's genuinely scary.

All this makes people angry. Repeat this rhetoric over and over again, getting them to believe it, and you can ramp up the blame game. That's why people become racist and homophobic, because they see the wrong things or are shown the wrong things. They are taught only to think of themselves. So if you're white, you become predisposed against people from black, Asian and ethnic minority groups. And if you're straight, you don't think about the travails of the LGBTQ+ community.

I never understood, if you're standing on the edge of a cliff and you don't know how big the drop is, why people would want to jump if someone told them to. I never got that. If you don't know what's down there, why jump when you can stay standing and do your best to find out for yourself? There might be a thousand fluffy mattresses, but what if there's a thousand crocodiles? Do you jump anyway and hope for the best? When you create a society of 'us against them', and you simultaneously make people's lives worse by blaming the people around them on the top of the cliff, they become incentivised to jump.

Education is the only answer, and it always will be. But it's harder and harder to educate people when they deliberately hold their hands over their ears after hearing what they want to hear. It's also increasingly difficult to educate them when everything is fractious – and kept fractious – because someone keeps stoking the flames. These people believe that they can build the society they want by breaking it first, and it's working.

I think there will be a lasting backlash against those who put self-interest over the well-being of others. People will question why a person who has access to millions of pounds continues to look after No. 1. We saw it with Mike Ashley at SportsDirect and Tim Martin, the idiot in charge of Wetherspoons. All of those famous chefs who forced their staff to take unpaid leave during the pandemic – how could you go to their restaurants and help make them more rich when it's all over?

If you're in a position where you have that much money and yet failed to look after your people, there have to be consequences – because you've played with the lives of others. Mike Ashley and Tim Martin are banking on the fact that there will always be a demand for cheap products, but they just don't care. They just refused to read the room.

The one that killed me the most was Richard Branson. That was just immoral. He was sat on his own island, worth billions, and yet he failed to realise that there was a time to put other people first. At a time like this, people want the team to succeed, whether it's their family, their local community or the country as a whole. They don't care about an individual losing one of their billions. So to do what Branson did is nothing short of scandalous.

I think the government must deal with these companies, and penalise those who failed to look after their staff. These people made massive money in the first place, but they have to feel the consequences of their greed and self-interest. Companies like SportsDirect have the country on a lead. People will need cheap clothes and sports equipment for their kids when this is over, and that's what they specialise in. If nothing is done, people like Mike Ashley will end up profiting from this whole mess. The government should have instructed the biggest businesses to look after their staff, and if they didn't then there ought to have been penalties. They have to stand up to these people.

The pandemic highlighted the real unsung heroes in our workforce. They're not the people at the top. They're those workers who the government labelled as unskilled, those they singled out to push through their agenda on immigration. It's the cleaners who went into hospitals every day, putting their health on the line for minimal pay because their job was necessary, and who get so little respect for their work. It's the teaching assistants who have very little job security, but who continue to help out despite funding cuts to education and youth centres.

We need to work out exactly who we value in society. We need to have a sensible conversation about the undervaluing of low-paid workers, without whom the system could not operate. And we need to take stock of what austerity did to this country while the rich were getting richer, and assess how many lives it cost. This is a time for real, meaningful change to create a fairer society.

Inequality

by Anne-Marie Silbiger

To understand inequality is to know that
*   equality is in our blood*
It travels through our veins
It spills the same path when injured
Our laughter rings in the same echoes
Our tears fall to the same soil in hope

15

LGBTQ+ ISSUES AND SEXUALITY

'LGBTQ+ people are just as worthy of your respect and understanding as anyone else. Take the time to listen to people's experiences and understand the challenges that they face.'
TransActual UK

I try to work out why people are so scared of difference. Sometimes I think it's just pure ignorance and a refusal to see another person's point of view; at other times I honestly just can't work it out. Perhaps there's a generation of people who simply can't get things in their heads because they haven't seen enough of life.

Kids today see everything on their mobile phones, with very few filters. It might seem a scary thought to most parents, but by the time they get to fourteen they've more or less seen everything. That, surprisingly, can have a very positive effect. It means that when they see or hear about a gay or bisexual kid, even at that age, most of them don't bat an eyelid.

These kids don't care. None of them care. But then there's a generation who are the opposite of that, who keep their stiff upper lip in place and think, 'I don't understand that, so it must be wrong.' People are small-minded because they've been indoctrinated to be that way, but they also aren't prepared to move outside of their small-mindedness.

I got a fair amount of stick when I first put trans people up on my Twitter account. People were accusing me of supporting human trafficking, prostitution, all sorts. But talk to them, like I do, and see what they have to say. If you still don't agree with them, then you still don't agree with them – but at least you'll have tried. The least you can do is find out, and the least you can then do is let them be without allowing your prejudice to show.

We have a problem in this country with false equivalence in the media. People are obsessed about balance because they're afraid of being accused of bias, even when a topic doesn't need balance. Some supposed scientist says one thing, and another scientist says something different. On the face of it, what they're both saying sounds reasonable. But at some point, somebody independent needs to come on and say, 'Well, actually, that person is right.'

There's also an acceptance of unpleasant attitudes, one that goes right to the top of the country. You've got Boris Johnson, a man who has said homophobic and racist things, and his only real explanation is that he was joking and his only punishment was to be made prime minister. Everything is just a joke to these people, because it doesn't matter to them. Boris, Nigel Farage and Tommy Robinson – they all have their deliberately divisive views and, sadly, they're all incredibly influential. If someone can be homophobic and racist and become the most powerful person in the country, it sends a message that such attitudes should be tolerated. But my view is that if you live in a tolerant society, which I believe everybody should want, you never automatically go against things, even if it's against your religion. Humanity has to be the only rule.

In fact, the struggles of the LGBTQ+ community formed a large part of my desire to educate myself further. It was almost a moment of enlightenment for me. We had a lad in school who wanted to come out as gay, and I realised that I didn't know what I was going to say to him. I went on Twitter, met some people, and they put me in touch with other people who gave me lots of advice and information. I still can't get all the acronyms right, though I do try. I spoke to one person who described themselves as 'Bi AF'. I was confused by that, so I asked them what 'AF' stood for. And they told me that it stands for 'as fuck'. You have to laugh! Right, that's me told.

During that time, I spoke to a woman who I think was living with another woman. Her mum is OK with her now, but they went through a difficult acclimatisation process. And I spoke to someone who had begun transitioning. These conversations persuaded me that if people could log on to my Twitter and talk openly about their feelings and what they have gone through, it would be a great opportunity to give them a voice.

The shit these people go through and the abuse they get from people is unbelievable. I spoke to someone high up in the fire service and told him about a person I know who was walking down the street when a fire engine drove past and someone shouted 'Tranny' out of the window. He agreed that it should never happen, but that's blindingly obvious and shouldn't even need to be said. Everyone has the right to be the person they want to be, as long as it doesn't impact upon other people. Who is someone else to stop you or make a judgement? If you aren't causing any harm, and are just going about your own business in the way you want to, why would anyone be a twat to you about it? Why can't we all be human to each other?

The same is true of sex workers. I used to think that sex work was just going onto street corners and waiting there – and for some people it is. Then I met a sex worker and started talking to her to educate myself. She travels all over the world, and she loves her job. And then there are sex workers who do it because they feel that they have no choice if they're going to feed their family. That's what helps to make it real. A few years ago, I spoke to a girl who had become a sex worker to put her son through private college and paid for all of that. In some people's eyes she'd be a bad mother. But I think, 'Fair play to you. You have a plan to make a better life for your kid.' She had problems with one of her clients but the police weren't interested because of how she earned her living. To some people, it's an industry that's easily vilified – or ignored. But in order to understand something, I think you've got to humanise it.

I also spoke to a girl in Nevada who signed a contract and then worked in a brothel. She's been doing it for two years because she has a business lined up. But she's discovered things about herself that enable her to be a good person, and this is her way of raising money to start her business. Others might do it to get through university. Another girl I spoke to works with a lot of disabled clients who can't go out. What's wrong with them having some pleasure, and who does that harm? If she goes to her clients' homes, speaks to them, hugs them and gives them some pleasure, that might help them feel better about themselves.

Everybody has their own way and their own reasons. When you get into what they want, it becomes a totally different world and you see things from a new angle. But imagine going out of the front door and not knowing who you're going to meet or whether you're going to get beaten up or abused. Some people say that in that case they shouldn't do it. But that's just the easy way out. These people pay taxes, so why don't they deserve some protection. It's not for other people to say that they shouldn't be doing it.

As with everything else, there has to be a grown-up conversation because it isn't going away. The approach at governmental level at the moment seems to be to ignore sex work and pretend that it doesn't happen, but plenty of politicians and civil servants use these services. Once sex workers band themselves together they'll become far stronger. The issues were highlighted by the coronavirus pandemic – what was done for sex workers? Nothing. Nothing at all. They were just ignored. These people had families to feed, they were looking after their families like everyone else, and yet there were no concessions made for them. They were the forgotten ones. But a society only functions properly if it protects its most vulnerable.

That's a whole section of society who have been washed down the drain. The government pretend they don't exist, yet there are thousands of them, and this might be their only way of making money. There's far worse people than them on the streets, believe me. If you want to stop the spread of a virus, think about how they get their work. By its very nature it's close contact, so they simply cannot operate. One of the most vulnerable groups of people in our society – and they're now left without a thing. What are they supposed to do?

When sex workers log on to my Twitter they generally get a really good response. Of course, you get the odd middle-aged person that gives them grief, but then that always happens. Those people think sex workers are all riddled with diseases, and that they're all bad parents. But that's because some people are knobheads, which is often nothing to do with the communities in which they exist. In certain sections of society, people use those knobheads as the figureheads or representatives of the community as a whole, because it gives them an explanation for their prejudice. The reality, outside of their intolerance, just isn't like that. When you speak to sex workers, what they tell you makes perfect sense. They explain the checks they get, how they pay their taxes and it all becomes clear. And then I can use that information to try to educate people who otherwise wouldn't have bothered to find it out. People make their own judgements, which are then set in stone. I suppose the difference with me is that I probably had some preconceptions too, but I was prepared for them to be wrong – and in many ways they were wrong.

I think that the sex-work industry is trying to come together, or at least recognise the power in sex workers doing so. In fact, I've been trying to get Unison to create a union for them. Because if I've got a million sex workers all under one umbrella, and I go to the government and tell them that we want better protection and better provisions, and if you don't do it we'll be voting en masse for the opposition, the government has to listen. When you come together, you give yourself

a voice. I think it's the only way to do it, and it's more important than anything – because nobody will look out for you
unless you do yourself.

For trans people, the same sort of process needs to happen
because of severe misinformation. You have high-profile
female sports stars spouting off that trans women aren't
women. And that view sticks with people. It's frightening. We
have to show these people the truth, and educate them.
There's a wilful ignorance, but those who are wilfully
ignorant do not let that stop them regurgitating their views.
You can't force someone to be trans, or force someone to be
gay. You can't have any surgery done until you are sixteen,
and you have to go through a period of counselling first.
There's someone I know who's been to Spain to have their
surgery because apparently that's one of the best places to go.
I wish people could see the journey that such people go
through just to be who they want to be. I know someone else
who has had the full change, and the difference in their
attitude, behaviour and confidence is astounding. Put simply,
they look, act and feel like the person they were always
supposed to be.

I've spoken to many trans people about their operations.
They have had their Adam's apples removed, their facial
bones shaved, their stomachs reduced. The people who say
that being trans is nothing but a choice, go out and speak to
these people. It isn't an easy choice to have all that done, to
go through voice coaching and risk being on the receiving end
of prejudice. People say it's easy, but that's absolute nonsense.
The lengths these people go to be the people they are is incredible, and it's fascinating.

Imagine walking into an office one day as a woman and saying, 'This is who I am.' Imagine the courage that takes. And then, in addition, imagine going through significant medical procedures. I believe that some people are simply born into the wrong shell. It has to happen; why wouldn't it, when everything else happens?

The biggest barrier to going through the transition is the potential impact on mental health. Trans people might struggle every day with the conundrum about whether to do it or not. There's the motivation of making the commitment to being who you want to be, but it's mitigated by the knowledge of what you have to go through to get there – and even after you've got there.

I think the first hurdle is the mental battle trans people face when deciding they should go through with – or continue to go through with – the process. When you're going to transition, there's so many things that you have to think about every day, and it's clearly a huge undertaking. They might start wearing different clothes, perhaps, or experimenting with make-up. But imagine if you were a woman in a man's body. Imagine how many different things you'd have to learn in order to feel like the routine was natural to you. And consider how hard it would be until the process *had* become natural.

Where do I get shoes? What will I wear? What hairstyle will I have? Which make-up suits me best? Do I need to think about how I walk and talk? Can I continue to play organised sport like I used to? How much will the whole process cost? If I transition into a woman, will I be paid less for my work? There's simply not enough information out there. All of those practical considerations can be barriers. It's really difficult. It's a daily struggle, just to be you.

There's also the stigma around it, and family and friends to take into consideration. What are your parents going to think? Your sisters, brothers, extended family, friends? How are your colleagues at work going to respond? These concerns are a daily problem before beginning the transition, during the transition and for a long while after the transition. Foreseeing being treated differently or badly at work is a huge barrier. Another is affordability. Because there are no grants available, it's all self-financed – and it's extremely expensive.

Once you make that commitment, it doesn't get any easier. You'll have bigots and the ignorant telling you that what you're doing is wrong, and some of them may be closer to home than you think. I've spoken to a couple of people who are transitioning and haven't spoken to their parents for two or three years. They've been cut off from their families. Surely if their families truly loved them they wouldn't care. There are really nice stories too, but there are some that make you wonder what goes through people's minds. Surely you just want your kids to be happy in any way they can? Be successful if they can be, but mainly just be happy. And if there was any time in our lives to realise that contentment is the one true aim, however it may come, it's now.

If you have a child and they told you they wanted to transition, how couldn't you be anything other than incredibly proud of them? Just think about the courage and mental strength it's taken them to even tell the people closest to them about who they really are. How much have they gone through simply to get to that point? Just getting to the stage of announcing your intention takes a huge leap, especially if there's a dad who when he sees someone gay on TV starts pointing his finger and coming out with homophobic slurs. It's then going to be much harder for the kid and will all become suffocating, meaning that they'll want to keep it hidden for fear of a negative reaction and being ostracised by their family. The chances of this leading to severe mental health issues are considerable – parents' attitudes and tolerance make a massive difference.

And then extend all this to your friends. And then extend it even further, to going into work and telling them that you want to be called something new. You're still the same person, but the treatment you receive from others might well change. You know people are going to stare at you, that they'll question your life choices and say, 'Yeah, but you're not really a woman/man, are you?' Think about the looks you'll get, and the number of eyes you'll feel boring into you.

There's a lot of people who spend their lives trying to stop people transitioning, and that's so dispiriting and it makes it all so daunting. Trans people just want to be who they want to be, without harming anyone. Imagine how isolated and alone you'd feel if people judged you for that simple desire. Mentally it must be exhausting. It takes a lot of bravery and nerve, and that bravery must be incredibly tiring. Unless you've gone through the process, you simply can't know how wearing it can be.

There are people who actively take against the trans community, and I honestly believe that they're evil. And then there are people who probably just don't understand it. But rather than explore and open themselves up to being educated, they close themselves off to it. I think it's one of those subjects that's surrounded by such a stigma both because of the lack of true information and the abundance of misinformation. There seems to be a growing hate among certain people for the community, hate that's becoming febrile.

So it's not just the ignorance of who trans people are, it's the ignorance of what they have to go through on a daily basis. On mental health issues, I think there's been a huge step forward in terms of the recognition of problems and the need to help people along the path. But the trans community still suffers from old-fashioned attitudes that just haven't caught up.

I think everybody makes a judgement with their eyes first, and that's the root of the problem. People judge others on what they look like. If you could see inside someone and see their personality, their heart and their soul, it would be much easier because you'd see the real person. Unfortunately, people make their minds up on basis of externals, on the shell. Anything different from the prescriptive 'normal', and people stare. It's embarrassing. I'd rather say, 'Tell me your story,' and let me know what's going on in your life.

LGBTQ+

by Anne-Marie Silbiger

I am you; I am him
I am her; I am them
I am a passing stranger
I am everyone you love

16

MENTAL HEALTH

'Situations trigger thoughts. Thoughts trigger feelings. Communicating our thoughts helps us find a perspective, and change the way we feel.'
Philippa Davies,
oursam.org.uk

One of the biggest issues in the mental health fight is that people have a pre-set idea of what 'normal' is. What's normal in your house might be different to what's normal in someone else's. That doesn't make you weird, or flawed – it just makes you different. Some people are able to be happy-go-lucky and optimistic, others aren't. That doesn't make either of them right or wrong, just different.

Unless you're willing to understand that other people work on different levels of normality, things will inevitably pass you by. You become blinkered. If you're not struggling with mental health issues, you allow yourself to assume that nobody else is, either around you or in society in general. You're helping to create a culture in which care and empathy are lacking. That's how people's mental health issues become exacerbated and why they can end up having dark thoughts – because people only consider their own sphere of normality.

I just wish people could spend a single day living through these people's experiences – understanding the confusion, the pain, the doubt, the rollercoaster of emotions; suffering the uncertainty of not knowing how each day will pan out, whether the dark clouds will gather over their mind. It must be an incredibly traumatic process for people to go through. If people had even a brief glimpse into that life, it would give them a different perspective on mental health and completely shift the conversation.

There's an incorrect assumption that depression and other serious mental health issues are synonymous with sadness – but someone suffering from depression can laugh and smile just like a non-sufferer can cry or be sad. Instead, things often just feel hopeless. Energy levels can drop, self-esteem evaporates, sleep can be problematic and appetite falls away. In this way, the symptoms of mental health issues can be as damaging as the issues themselves, because the process becomes a vicious cycle: the issues lead to the symptoms, and the symptoms exacerbate the issues.

There was a video I saw recently on Twitter of a guy naked in the street. It was shared because people thought he was pissed, but that conclusion came through their own view of normal. In fact, the guy had severe mental health issues. But people didn't immediately realise this. Someone with mental health issues might have spotted it, but the majority couldn't because it was outside their own world view. This makes it really difficult at times to put your finger on mental health issues. Obviously, if you see your best mate every other day or your child all day, every day, you might notice a change in their behaviour and reach out to them.

But even then they might have found mechanisms for hiding it.

What I'm looking for is what people don't say, and the reactions and emotions they don't have. You can ask someone if they're OK, and they might say, 'Yeah, I'm fine,' but how have they said it? How do they look? Why haven't they expanded upon that answer? Why haven't they messaged you recently? Why haven't they been to the pub with the lads for the usual get-togethers for a while? Do they look a bit more scruffy, when normally they dress smartly? Does their house look a little unkempt? Are they sleeping on the sofa when their bed is just upstairs? But unless you go looking for these signs, it's easy to miss them.

You might ask them again and they'll say, 'Yeah, but ...' or 'Well, yeah, I suppose,' and that gives you clues that you can use. Sometimes you might push it further, and other times you might just make a mental note to check in on them more than you usually would.

It might be easy to spot the clues in a close friend or family member, but it's a lot harder if it's a more distant friend or even someone that you just talk to through work or on social media. But that only means that you have to be more attentive; there are so many things that you just won't spot unless you're looking for them.

It can be extremely difficult speaking to people at their lowest ebb. The other week I got a message from someone asking me to ring a guy who was very ill. They were an Everton supporter and long-term season ticket holder, and they were dying from terminal cancer and wanted to speak to one of their footballing heroes. I said I'd do it, obviously. A few hours later, I got another message to say that they'd spoken to the doctors and the guy was on his way out and didn't have long. He might make it through the night, but they understandably wanted me to ring sooner rather than later.

I picked up the phone, but what do you say to someone in that position? I started by saying, 'All right, mate?' as if it were a normal conversation, and then immediately apologised because it was a stupid thing to say. I chatted to him and his wife for a while, but it was exceedingly difficult. They were both obviously incredibly emotional and upset. But afterwards his wife said that it did make him smile, which is great. Phone calls like that put everything into perspective.

I've read a lot of books by people who have gone through periods of suffering from anxiety. They describe it like a tap coming from a fuel tank that produces so much anxiety, much more than a typical person might have. It's very hard to get rid of the tank when it's full. So you have to ease the issue by emptying that anxiety tank drip by drip, dribble by dribble. Only once the tank is empty can you remove it completely.

It was inevitable that the coronavirus crisis exacerbated problems with anxiety and mental health for the most vulnerable. Imagine if you live in a place you hate, or with a person that abuses you, or in an environment that makes you unhappy. The impact of lockdown and social distancing will be greatly magnified. That can make life suffocating. Going outdoors and enjoying the freedom that doing so brings is a really effective way of releasing anxiety and tension, and having that restricted can exacerbate mental health issues, while also making you potentially more disconnected from the people who can help you.

Everything became a cycle of negativity. Everything on social media and on TV understandably became skewed towards the virus, but it was all negative. We were having the number of cases and deaths fed to us every day. We were hearing about the struggles of doctors and nurses on an hourly basis, and how the system wasn't built soundly enough to cope. Football supporters lost the chance to go and watch their team, which for many is a yardstick of social normality. This only exacerbated all the negativity that they might already have been feeling. It was a time during which even the most mentally resilient people were worrying more than ever before, and with good reason. But if you were already lonely or low, imagine what this was doing to you. These people weren't seeing any positivity.

The biggest thing about Covid-19 was that everything seemed so uncertain, so unknown, and there wasn't a definite end date. When would we get over the worst? When would it come back? Would I survive if I got it? Would there ever be a universal vaccine or might the virus perhaps mutate? If you're going through something shit but you've got an end date, you can reason with it and focus on that. But this had no certainty to it. It was all totally alien to us, and that was incredibly dispiriting for some people.

It didn't help that we had a prime minister who seemed incapable of delivering a coherent and consistent message. First it was herd immunity, then it was lockdown. He tried to answer questions and it was just embarrassing. First it was not testing, then it was a huge rush to test people. He was preaching a message of staying at home and social distancing, but before that he was boasting about shaking hands with everyone. He and the cabinet clearly weren't social distancing, because many of them caught it, and he had a pregnant girlfriend at home. What sort of message did that send?

I don't believe that being a professional footballer, even a successful one with the pressures that come with it, makes you any more likely than anyone else to suffer severe mental health issues. Footballers might be more prone to the addictions that sometimes provoke these issues, but even then I'm sceptical. I don't think that it's true to say that there's something about being a footballer that makes depression more likely.

Mental illness doesn't choose people. It doesn't discriminate between rich or poor, successful or struggling, footballer or any other job. That's just not how it works. Of course, the environment in which someone operates might sometimes exacerbate mental health issues, but psychological difficulties are universal.

I don't think that there's any rhyme or reason to it, really. Some people will show signs of mental illness, perhaps because they're more expressive, or perhaps just because that's how they happen to react. Some people will have severe mental health issues, and yet nobody ever realises because they manage to keep them buried deep within themselves.

It was a horrible, tragic shock when Gary Speed passed away. There was never any sign that it was coming, and that can be the scariest part of mental illness. You just never know what's around the corner until it's too late. I still find it hard to believe that Gary is gone. I sometimes forget now, thinking that at some point he'll walk into the room at a Wales game and I'll be able to have a chat with him again. I think that this suggests that he's still there in some form, in my memories of him. Gary was a person whose impact upon people will last forever, and so many of the people he played with or managed would say exactly the same.

Gary was a perfectionist. He was always chasing the chance to improve, and never settled for anything other than being the best. Maybe that element of his personality might have caused anxieties to build up inside, ones that he was afraid to confront. But think backwards, using hindsight, and you can analyse everything in an attempt to find reasons for someone's behaviour. I don't really know whether it's helpful or not.

There was another lad I played with who also committed suicide: Alan Davies. Alan was a Welsh lad who started at Manchester United and then played for Swansea, but I played a few times for Wales with him. He died in 1992. He was only thirty.

Sadly, suicide is now one of those things where most people know someone who has taken their own life, or a friend of a friend. It's the biggest killer of men of a certain age, and there must be an explanation for that. Society doesn't help, and it's not controversial to say that life feels shit for a lot of people at the moment. But there are a million and one different reasons.

One of the most difficult things to compute is that you can't really tell if someone is happy or sad just by looking at them – or even by talking to them. They might be smiling and talkative on the outside, but this could be a mask that they've learnt to use to avoid having to open up and address their issues. Someone can laugh all day long and still suffer from depression.

We need to reinforce the message that it's OK to feel shit. That feeling shit is completely normal. That we understand that you feel shit. That we want to help you feel less shit. But that even if we do say all this, there will still be days afterwards when you feel shit. All that people with mental illness want is for someone – for society – to put them in their arms and hold them. And if they do want to talk, they don't want to be told that they can't see anyone today and to come back in three weeks.

The problem is that too many people still don't take mental health seriously. Take Piers Morgan. How can he get away with telling people with mental health issues to 'man up'? He had a go at Raheem Sterling too about his tattoo, but didn't have any idea about the context. If I'd been Sterling, I'd have worn a T-shirt with a picture of Morgan and a drawing of a cock.

Morgan is another symptom of the modern media disease. People give him credit for saying what he thinks, but he doesn't say what he thinks; he says what he thinks will make him notorious and create headlines. He's not stupid – he knows exactly what he's doing – yet somehow he presents breakfast TV and is held up as a celebrity.

He's got children, and I wonder if they think that he's a knobhead. At least when he's on TV they get a break from him. But look at ITV – they're the ones to blame. They give him a platform from which to spout offensive things on trans issues and mental health because they value his notoriety above everything else. And why give Nigel Farage or Katie Hopkins radio shows? Because you prioritise ratings over morality. 'Ooh, these people say what they think.' Well, so fucking what?

There's a time to be critical and a time to be kind, and mocking people on trans issues when you've got a platform on national TV isn't the way to behave. But as long as he's Marmite, he doesn't care a jot. That's the behaviour of a bully, shouting louder than everyone else. But the louder people shout, the less knowledge they have. Morgan was at the forefront of the debate about the government's reaction to the coronavirus pandemic, but he only says what he believes will make him notorious and newsworthy.

I know that the 'man up' culture did exist in football at one time, that you had to be a man's man to survive. When I walked into the dressing room, I was told that I shouldn't show any fear or show that I was hurt, as it would be an admission of weakness. Looking back, that was so unhelpful. But now, with different cultures and different attitudes in dressing rooms, I think it's become easier for players to open up and say something. The public's reaction would be completely different to how it would have been thirty years ago. And, of course, the increasing use of psychologists within clubs is absolutely crucial too. They should be picking up on signals that others may miss, whether at home or within the club itself. Football is a pressured environment, and some players struggle to ease that pressure. If you're unable to ease it, it builds up until it becomes unmanageable.

That culture around men, the 'man up' philosophy of Piers Morgan, is incredibly irresponsible. It suggests that your state of mind is a choice, as if it's something that people can make decisions about. And this in turn implies that those who suffer from mental health problems should in some way assume responsibility for having those issues. When Morgan says 'man up', it shows exactly what he thinks about mental health.

But because he's on mainstream TV, he's influential. People start to believe the things he says. They think that because he's been employed by one of the main broadcasters, there must be some truth to his comments. It's one thing attracting attention by chatting shite about vegan sausage rolls or whatever, but another thing entirely when you attack the trans community or tell people with depression to 'man up'. He's got a responsibility to be better than that. That's unforgivable, no matter how many times he tries to reinvent himself.

I'd love to take some of those people who believe in 'man up' and give them the same money as footballers. Here's £5 million a year, and here's all that media intrusion, here's that pressured environment, here's working constantly on your fitness and knowing that a serious, career-ending injury might be around the corner, here's all the abuse at matches and online, here's all those vultures hanging around you looking for a piece of you. Let's see how they cope. There's a good reason why Camelot offers counselling to National Lottery winners.

The biggest myth of mental illness is that money, fame and success are a barrier against it. They're not. There's no injection, no VIP pass that you can buy. It creeps into people and it breaks them, if they're unable to get help. You can step out of your mansion, drive around in your Bentley, play golf every day, visit luxury locations all over the world on holiday, eat in the most exclusive restaurants, drink the best wines, and have a loving family and friends – and you can still be the loneliest person in the world. The one thing you can't escape is your own mind. You can still feel shit with all of that.

Success and fame can act like a trap. You live in a world where certain things are expected of you as standard, yet you feel unable to handle it. Once you become a footballer, the one thing you've got to give up is freedom. While you're playing, wherever you go, people have mobile phones and can take pictures of you. Everything you do can be documented. That takes away some of your liberty. You also have a whole host of people hanging around you, wanting to take things from you. The number of agents that used to try to get money, make money or grab a piece of me was astonishing, and it must be ten times worse nowadays. If everyone knows you're paid £100,000 a week, there will always be people lurking around, after a bit of the action. There are vultures spread wide across the game, ready to pick at you.

That's a hard thing to deal with. How do you know who to trust? People are trying to sell you cars, houses or business ventures just to get their commission – so are they in it for you or for themselves? Maybe you worry that your agent is trying to engineer a move or a bumper new contract so that they can take their cut. Maybe you become suspicious that potential romantic partners desire you just for your money. Maybe that makes you only trust yourself, and maybe that makes you lonely and vulnerable. You lose control of elements of your life, and even if you identify someone who isn't healthy for you and cut them loose, there will be a long line of others trying to do the same. It can become a vicious cycle.

I once had an agent who owed me ten grand and he came to see me. He drove to the house in a huge Mercedes estate, while I was still driving my club Volvo. He said that he couldn't pay me back, that he had taken the money out of my account and needed to use it. He said that two months earlier he'd declared himself bankrupt, so there was no obligation to pay me. I asked if he could give me his Mercedes, and he said that it was registered in his wife's name. His other car was in her name too, and his house. So I couldn't do anything.

There was also an Irish fella who owed me some money, and I asked for it back. He said that he couldn't send it from Ireland, because he wasn't allowed to. I laughed and said that he could send me a cheque, but again he said he couldn't do that. Eventually, he just stopped replying to my messages and I never heard from him again. For every well-meaning person around a player, there's at least two up to no good.

I always managed to stay grounded. I went to live back in Llandudno, surrounded by virtually the same people as before. Some people did treat me differently and couldn't fathom that I hadn't changed, but I still talked the same, behaved the same, did the same things – so I was still me. But I think that's much harder now with the money in the game.

The potential benefits of a modern footballer's lifestyle are obvious, but it depends what sort of person you are. If you're happy to engage with people, get stopped in public, be gregarious and embrace your fame, it might suit you perfectly. But if all you wanted was to be the best footballer you could be and are happy being a quiet, family person, you might get mis-sold as sulky or miserable. Some people just want to walk their dog and not talk to anyone.

One coping mechanism that I recognised in teammates was to have two personas: one on the pitch and another away from it. Pat Van Den Hauwe was one of the most aggressive players you could face on the pitch, but off it he was incredibly shy. Pat could walk into the room now and feel awkward about talking to me, and I know him well. But he played a character on the pitch. Duncan Ferguson was the same. He isn't an aggressive man, he's shy too. When he knows you he's great, but he's reserved at first. Mark Hughes also – quiet and gentle off the pitch. But on it, all these guys had this hyper-aggressive personality. Perhaps they played a character on the pitch because it helped them to be better footballers, but it also allowed them to be two different people. When Duncan was on the pitch he was Duncan Ferguson the player, and off it he was Duncan Ferguson the person. That might have enabled him to have a more normal life. There's some sense in it, I think.

There are also several things that can happen in a player's career that can affect their mental health. You can never think about serious injury for long, because if you did you'd never play to your full potential. If you're fearful of getting hurt, you wouldn't go into challenges in the right way. But then not thinking about serious injury means that you might be unable to adequately prepare for the mental anguish of it. And that can be devastating. Imagine training all your life to be a striker, making the grade and being successful, and then doing your cruciate ligaments at the age of twenty-three. You don't know how long you'll be out for or if you'll even be able to come back as strong. The physical side of the injury is only one part of it.

It also depends at what point in your career the injury comes. Norman Whiteside signed for Everton and did OK, but then his knee went and his career was over. Norman had already achieved a lot, he got a good insurance pay-out and so he was able to be pretty philosophical about it. But what happens if you're fifteen and you break your leg badly in academy football? Where's the support for that? You're only just learning how good you could be, and you might be done. Even if you come back, you've missed so much football that younger players have caught you up.

When I was out for six months with my most serious injury, it was hard. But I knew I could come back, and I knew early on that it wouldn't be a career-ender. That obviously helps, because it gives you something to focus on. But if you live in a bubble, and that bubble bursts in an instant, you have to start a new life. And it's damn hard. At that point, there's not much difference between a footballer and a factory worker who's been told that their job no longer exists. You both have skills that might now be of little use in your everyday life.

People seem to assume that footballers are superhuman, that they're somehow immune to the rigours of life. But we're not. We're ordinary people who happen to be good enough at something that society is obsessed by. That obsession leads to players being placed on pedestals that they didn't ask for and judged by a different set of rules. We live life like anyone else. We're as fallible as anyone else, maybe more so given the trappings that can come with it. We make mistakes like anyone else. We might fly high in a sporting context, but that means nothing in the context of real life. And we're neither invincible nor immortal. The death of Gary Speed, and the subsequent passing of other players and managers I've known and worked with, hammers that home.

I want to end this chapter with a piece of advice on self-care that I believe is incredibly important, and perhaps sometimes overlooked. One of the biggest problems in the treatment of mental health issues is that some of the people who are best prepared to help others are those who suffer – or have suffered – mental health issues themselves. But in taking on the burden of helping others (and I use the word 'burden' without any pejorative sense), they threaten their own mental health.

Everybody needs to protect themselves in order to help others. You have to be in the right place to help. At a time such as the coronavirus pandemic, lots of people were prepared to give and give, and that's great, but it took its toll on them because they were unable to protect themselves. I consider myself to be a very content person, but I have to protect myself. I'll pull back out of Twitter if I need to, even if it's only an hour, three hours or an entire day – whatever I need to do. I listen to the people around me who tell me that I need to ensure I'm looking after myself. In the great scheme of things, I'm fine. I've a house, I've enough food, I can watch any old shit on TV that takes my fancy, I can have a nap if I want. But you still have to make sure to self-care.

If you have a child that suffers from anorexia, you'll be worn out. If your wife or husband has mental health issues, you'll be worn out. It's really hard to get away from anything. The first port of call for anyone in this world is to look after themselves. I don't mean in terms of money or possessions, but their well-being. Only after they've done that should they try to help others.

It takes a level of emotional maturity to recognise this. Nobody's a superhero. Nobody can just carry on giving forever without getting damaged by the experience, both physically and mentally. And if you continue down that path without considering your own self-care, the level of care you can give to others diminishes. That's important to remember. To be the best carer you can be to others, you've got to take care of yourself. To get the right balance between quality and quantity is very difficult, because you might want to help as many people as possible. But you have to make it work for you.

Mental health

by Anne-Marie Silbiger

Mental health is physical health
We must stop separating the two
Hold them in regard
as one

17

GETTING OLD

'Let us never know what old age is. Let us know the happiness time brings, not count the years.'
Ausonius, Roman poet,
fourth century AD

We're afraid to enjoy ourselves as a country, or are apologetic for trying to do so. Everyone is so dour and aloof. Bring out the bits of your personality that you enjoy, because other people will enjoy them too. Because educating and connecting with people is about inspiration, and it's impossible to inspire people if you can't excite them. Maintaining that excitement as you get old and your body starts to grow weary can be incredibly difficult.

I only ever wanted to play for Everton because I considered it to be my home. If we'd never won anything that might have changed, but being successful allowed me to stay there and in doing so feel like I was coming into a second home every day. Nowhere else ever felt like that.

I always wanted to be at a club that matched my ambition and I'd have become disillusioned if I ever thought that Everton didn't have the same attitude as me. People seem to think that it's acceptable to say, 'Well, if we get in the top four or the top six, we've done well,' but I'd never agree with that. That only produces an 'Oh well, never mind' ethic that actively makes success less likely. It teaches you to be satisfied with something less than the best.

If you tell yourself that you're not going to win something, then you won't. I hate it when people say that Everton will have done well if they finish in the top ten. What message does that give to the players? That if they finish eighth, everyone will be happy – so don't bust a gut to push harder for more? That just good enough is good enough?

You listen to Howard Kendall, Alex Ferguson and Kenny Dalglish interviews from when they were in charge in the 1980s and 1990s, and if their team lost a game they rushed to praise the opponents. They sold a message that the opposition must have played extraordinarily well to beat their brilliant side. It reinforced the principle that only by being exceptional could anyone beat their team. They might say that it was only injuries or bad refereeing that could stop them. Now, in the dressing room they might tear strips off the players, but the message was always positive.

But eventually the positivity runs out for every player at every club. When the end of my Everton career came, it was pretty unpleasant. In October 1997 I was restored to the starting XI for the Merseyside derby after being dropped for two matches – Paul Gerrard had played in 4–1 League Cup defeat to Coventry City and was at fault for three goals. We beat Liverpool 2–0, with teenager Danny Cadamarteri scoring a brilliant goal. If I thought that was a turning point for me, I was wrong. We took one point from our next six league matches, scoring only three times, including five straight defeats, ending with a 2–0 home loss to Tottenham that kept us bottom of the league. After the Tottenham game, hundreds of supporters stayed after the final whistle at Goodison to protest at how the club was being run.

The following week we travelled to Leeds, and I assumed that I would keep my place. I hadn't actually done much wrong during that awful run; we were just playing badly as a team. But on the morning of the match, Howard Kendall asked to see me. He told me that after a great deal of deliberation he was leaving me out of the team. I wasn't the type of person to rant and rave at the manager, because there was clearly no way that I was going to change Howard's mind. I believed that it would have been hard to give someone like me that news, and he wouldn't have gone through it all to be immediately dissuaded by me. Thomas Myhre played instead, and he did really well in a 0–0 draw.

What hurt most was how Howard's treatment of me changed completely from then on. When I went into training on the following Monday, he told me that I was no longer going to train with the first team, the reserves or the academy kids. I was effectively no longer welcome at the training ground. I had a meeting with him in which he asked if I wanted to be the goalkeeping coach on a fraction of my wage, but I told him I needed to go elsewhere and play. Eventually, he gave me permission to seek a new club.

After sixteen years of being at one club, that might seem like an unfair way to be treated. But I don't think it was anything personal towards me from Howard. That's just how he was. Once he'd made his decision, that was it. And he dealt with things in such a way that one day you were in his circle, the next you were on the outside looking in. I'd seen it happen to other players. This was just my turn. But the rejection still hurt me badly. I loved Everton, and still do, but I never wanted to be at a club where I knew I wasn't wanted. All I wanted to do was play football, and if that wasn't going to happen at Everton then I needed to fight for it to happen somewhere else.

I also couldn't just stay away from the training ground. It wasn't in my character to simply accept my fate and sit around at home. I could have avoided training completely, but I was still in every day working my bollocks off, desperate to prove Howard wrong. It was also a way of pissing him off, by refusing to just slope away, which is probably what he would have liked me to do.

I eventually got loan moves to Southend United and Stoke City, which with Southend involved me commuting from North Wales to spend Thursday, Friday and Saturday there and then travel home. Both clubs had a good atmosphere and I was grateful for the opportunities to keep playing. I eventually joined Stoke permanently. But nothing quite felt like Everton, which was tough to deal with mentally. No matter how hard people tried, nowhere was ever really like home, as I'd lost the deep emotional connection with a football club that I was lucky to enjoy at Goodison. Most players know that loyalty can be a flimsy concept in football, but at Everton I truly believed that the club had the same commitment to me as I had to them.

I mourned the loss of Everton in my life. When you're tied to one club, experiencing the ups and downs that it enjoys and endures as if they're your own, you devote yourself to that club. Everton weren't just my employers, they were a large part of me. Removing my opportunity to play for them provoked a loss of confidence and feelings of rejection, just as if it had been a long-term relationship that ended suddenly.

Like someone who has come out of a long-term relationship, I then bounced around a few short-term options as I tried unsuccessfully to replicate what I'd felt at Everton. My time at Torquay United was the most enjoyable of these, and I was named their Player of the Year in 1998/99 as we avoided relegation to the Conference. I was playing well and, crucially, had found a place where I was truly wanted. It also helped that I didn't dwell on the level that I used to play at. I never thought of myself as different because I'd played for my country and at the highest level in the club game. Of course, the facilities were different, training on a field that we used to call Dogshit Park. But I was treated exactly the same as anyone else, and paid about the same as everyone else. I just turned up and played, and playing was all I ever wanted.

Later on, it became pretty clear pretty quickly that I wasn't suited to being a football manager. I managed Hastings United in the Ryman League, a part-time job that I combined with other roles, and had a caretaker manager job at Margate. But I didn't really enjoy this sort of work, as it seemed to be based on principles that I wasn't comfortable with. After all, I've never been afraid to cause a stir. If I believe in what I'm saying, I have no problem with challenging authority and provoking a debate or discussion. I see absolutely no point in being a yes man if I don't agree with the yes. As long as I can look back and say that I stayed true to what I believe in, then I can hold my head up high. But the moment you start making decisions based on what someone else thinks, there's really no point in doing the job.

Football management for me was never a stable job. In the lower leagues you're forced to work amid constant change, and with all manner of backroom and boardroom instabilities. You aren't so much managing a football team as fighting fires and overseeing crises. And then you get judged solely on results, despite all the noise going on around you that only makes your job more difficult.

I think that I was also destined to struggle because of who I was as a player. Football management in England is largely based on an 'old boys' network, which means the same managers get the same jobs and take the same staff and the same old ideas with them. I tended to do my own thing during my career, slightly separated from the group. That was partly because I was a goalkeeper, and partly because of my personality and way of working, but it didn't lend itself to being part of that network.

It never stopped me from becoming a goalkeeping coach, however, and I'm very proud of what I achieved in that role. I improved a number of goalkeepers that I worked with, and believe I would probably still be able to do the same now. But I've also made peace with the fact that I was seen as slightly alternative, something that played against me in football, although it enabled me to start this new life, one that makes me just as – if not more – proud. I never wanted my playing career to end, and that was no secret. I would have played on forever if I could. I was lucky that as a goalkeeper you have greater longevity than outfield players, so I managed to extend

it into my forties. But you quickly learn that you don't retire
– the game retires you.

I was disappointed with the way it ended at Everton, but I
could see from their point of view why they were happy for
me to move on. I still thought that I had plenty to give, but
wherever else I went it just didn't feel like home, even if I was
playing well. Dropping down the leagues helped me match
the decline in the standard of my play, so I never got to the
stage where I thought that I was letting people down or
becoming less useful. But as a person, emotionally, none of my
subsequent clubs ever gave me the feeling I'd always enjoyed
at Everton.

I was playing at Torquay, and the travelling was really
hard. We played a match away at Chester, and I got a concus-
sion and was seeing double for some of the game. Afterwards,
the manager told me that my performance wasn't good
enough and that I wasn't wanted by the club anymore. But
he couldn't do it to my face; he waited and did it over the
phone. That got to me, and I realised that the time had come
to stop.

I was fortunate that I quickly got into coaching, because
that provided a link between playing and the real world,
easing the impact of losing football as an everyday part of
my life. I could have stayed on at Everton as the goalkeeping
coach a few years before retiring, but as I've mentioned that
would have meant reducing my wages significantly – and I
thought that if I was going to do that, then I'd rather keep
playing elsewhere and experience life at other clubs. It was
another way of making that eventual step to retirement
easier, because I was stepping outside my Everton bubble. I

didn't think that Howard Kendall would stay long anyway, which might have meant me losing my job too, and I wouldn't have been able to deal with all the club politics stuff easily either.

My acclimatisation to retirement was easier not just because I always felt quite grounded as a person, but because I'd done other jobs too. In my early years as a player I'd worked on building sites and been a binman, so I knew what life was like outside football and wasn't afraid to get my hands dirty. So it was less a jump into the unknown, and more a step back into what I used to know. It was as simple as thinking, 'Right, I better find something else to do.'

But for some players, and more so now than when I played, I can imagine that it's incredibly hard to lose that structure and the only career they've known, then immediately focus on something different. We never really had that conversation as older senior professionals about what came after football – we were so focused on the next game, and I also suspect that some of us just didn't want to think about it. As a footballer, you're taught to be exclusively focused on the next week and the next match, rather than further down the line. You know the cliché: take each game as it comes. But that's how foot-ballers think. If you go any further than that, you take your eye off the present. If a new manager came in, you might worry about your place at the club, but other than that you just lived day to day, week to week.

What this can mean is that you suddenly reach an age where retirement is nearing, and you've never stopped to think long term. It might well be different now with the money in the game, but there was very little support for retiring players. I know plenty will have had ideas about starting a business or running a pub or might have paid well into their pensions, but it's still a scary thing to face.

The only possible regrets that I had were that I had an offer from Chelsea that Everton refused to let me accept because they said I was needed at Goodison (despite them making it clear not long after that I was free to leave), and also that I never played abroad. Bayern Munich were keen at one point, but then I was so happy at Everton that I can't really say that I was upset about it. Maybe I wouldn't have liked London or Germany. Maybe those places wouldn't have felt like home either.

I certainly didn't have a plan when I was playing, and I don't even have one now, really. I tend to live in the moment and never think two or three years into the future. It's just not me. I concentrate on the now and see what happens. Of course, there's things that I want to do in my life, but that's probably just an age thing and realising that I probably need to crack on with them.

For me it was just a case of doing what I had to, but I never said no to anything, which meant that my days immediately after finishing playing were always full. For a time I was driving from my house in Chester to Bradford City to train the goalkeepers there in the morning, then driving to York City and training their goalkeepers in the afternoon. Then I'd drive back to Bradford and do the academy, before driving home and getting in at 10pm. That might be three days per week, plus wherever I was on a Saturday with the team. But I didn't mind that. It kept a structure in place while I worked out what I wanted to do.

It might sound a bit nonsensical, given the money that players earn – although not when I played, I should say – but one of the biggest worries for any retiring player is financial. You're a long time retired, and if you've become used to a certain way of life and haven't saved enough, that can be a very hard thing to cope with.

There should be an obligatory clause written into young players' contracts that a certain percentage of it, as standard, goes into a pension pot that you can't touch until you retire. I'm sure plenty of players do get good advice and that this happens, but it should apply to all players. You're given your first £100,000, and a part of that is stowed away, because you don't even need £30,000 a week as a nineteen-year-old kid. When the next contract is signed you do the same, all the way up to twenty-five. As the money increases in the game, this only becomes more important. Every player should want to save for the future, but it's easy to live in the moment financially and put saving off because you're riding the crest of a wave. Retirement comes quickly.

There are two reasons for implementing this. First, at a young age it's very hard to manage your money. You possess incredible wealth compared with those around you, your family and friends, and you can end up squandering it on things you don't need because society insists you have to spend.

Second, you'll have people around you who – deliberately or not – give you bad advice that can cause your wealth to disappear. Even if that does happen, if some of the money is secured until after you finish playing, you still have a safety net. No Premier League player these days should be worrying about their financial future as it can cause mental health issues that affect performance.

Players might say that they can easily start a business when they retire, and they'll have loads of cash to do it that they should earn well into their thirties, but life moves in odd ways and there's no guarantee of anything. If you squirrel money away, you can be set up for the rest of your life and do genuinely good things with that money.

There's no doubt that having a high level of disposable income can make life more comfortable, but it can also make things more difficult. When you're a player you can't concentrate on anything else – you have to be fully focused. But wealth can easily be a distraction. You see players now getting involved in businesses in their early twenties, and you just want to shake them and tell them not to. If you're giving less than 100 per cent to either the game or your business, neither will work properly.

And so, without football, I threw myself into something else. The idea of helping others had always been attractive, and I was fortunate to be able to start a new life working with kids that really needed my help. It's never easy work, and there are times when it's bloody hard, but the feeling of being useful gives me as much satisfaction as football did.

I've always liked getting up early. Normally I get up at 5am during the week and try to get to school for 6.30am. I can start doing things there while it's quiet, and chat to the deputy head. Then from around 8.45am, I'm picking up kids and dropping them off at various places where they might have apprentice placements. I come back to school and start working on arranging future placements and other things around the school.

But I try to get out as much as I can. I'll drive somewhere to speak to someone about the work we do, and attempt to arrange as many placements as possible for the kids. Every day is different, and I really like that. At the weekend I'm happy staying within my own four walls, because they're *my* four walls, but during the week I prefer to be on the move and have a different agenda every day. I also like to go and meet people from mental health charities, or go to conferences and listen to people. I'm a union representative for Unison, so that involves some work too.

The philosophy of our school is to give the kids what they want, because that's the best way to help them. So if they want to work in a garage, we'll try to arrange as much of that experience as we can. If they want to work with animals, we'll try to get them helping on a farm. But this all takes planning, and it isn't easy. There's a perception that special schools have pupils who you don't want to deal with, and fighting against that can be problematic. Sometimes we'll have a really good run, and sometimes weeks will go by and we've been unable to get anything lined up.

I'll do whatever I can to get resources for the kids. I did a thing at Warwick Races for Poundland, and they gave us £3,000 worth of uniforms. All that sort of stuff gets me out on an afternoon. My boss is incredibly understanding, and he knows that I'm better getting out and making things happen. When I get home, I'll have a shower and some tea, then start talking to people on Twitter and trying to help them. I can have the TV on if it's quiet online, but sometimes it's busy and virtually non-stop. I'll normally go to bed at 9pm and read, or just stay on Twitter if it's busy.

I have tried to cut back on the Twitter stuff a little bit – but even when I try to do that, I have to keep checking in on people. I'm also aware that my follower count needs to stay high to make it all worthwhile. That's the trouble with Twitter. It never stops, which is why the takeovers are good – they give me some time off because the account is being used during those hours. I love Friday nights; the takeover starts at 9pm and I've said good night to everyone on there before that. I know I have Saturday, with as little to do on the social media side of things as possible.

There's also the chance that someone needs me urgently. I've sometimes woken up on a Saturday morning, intending to do nothing, but been messaged by someone at their lowest ebb who's having dark thoughts. How can I just say to them, 'Well, sorry, I was after a quiet day today'? Unfortunately, that's how life works. It doesn't fit an ideal schedule and it doesn't fit into your plans. But it's not a great thing to wake up to, and it's draining.

I guess there must just be something within me – and I don't know what it is – that makes people want to tell me stuff about themselves. When I went on the suicide course, they said I'd be a good counsellor, but I can't afford to lose me. I have to stay true to me. I can't be shaped to do things a certain way, because I think me being me is what makes people open up. And if I was struggling, I think I'd be able to call on people to support me in the same way. I'd want exactly the same, just to be listened to and understood on a human level.

The main thing that football taught me for this new life is how to prepare my body and mind for multiple tasks in a short period of time, and that's been a huge help. Football taught me to do something, then quickly put it away and move on. That's how I cope with doing lots of different tasks on the same day. When one thing is done, I can easily put it to one side, which clears my mind to move on to the next part of the day. Everything gets left at the door, and that makes it easier for me to break things down into manageable chunks. I can switch off very easily, and I'm sure that's down to football. I don't think I could do it any other way, or my brain would turn to mush.

One of the scariest things about getting old is losing people around you. It brings your own mortality into sharp focus. In 2012 Gary Ablett died after a long, brave battle against cancer, and Gary Speed had taken his life the previous year. Both of these were incredibly tough to take. I'd known them before they were players at Everton, and knew those close to them too. They were two of the nicest people you could ever hope to meet, and their passing hammers home how precious life is – and how indiscriminate death can be. Being a footballer might be the best job in the world, but it doesn't protect you from the horrors of cancer or mental illness.

When someone like Gary Speed or Gary Ablett dies, you lose something from the club, because even after they had left Everton, they remained a living part of it. They were symbols of how honest, hard-working and brave footballers can make such an extraordinary difference. These two were men of the people, and club men through and through. If we could all be like Gary Ablett and Gary Speed, the world would be a far better place.

Getting old

by Anne-Marie Silbiger

Getting old is smelling the rose I never noticed
  before
Growing in bushes I simply did not see
Sitting with my faults and quirks
Smiling contentedly

EPILOGUE
BE BETTER

I knew that I wanted to do something different when I retired from playing, as I don't think I was ever really committed to working within football as a coach or manager. The game has moved on in so many ways; it's so different now. I'd be happy to mentor young goalkeepers, but working with the first team just wasn't for me. I'm happy now, and that's the main thing.

I also didn't always want to be known as a footballer and then as a former footballer. It's one of my biggest bugbears. I go into schools now and get introduced as a former footballer. Yes, I used to play football, but I don't now and that's not why I'm here. That was then and this is now, so judge me on how I do my job, not on who I used to be. I find that annoying, always being the person that I was, not what I am.

It's very hard to start something new when people constantly label you as what you once were. When I get introduced at a conference as a former footballer I think, 'Who gives a fuck? I'm not here to stop shots and catch crosses for you.' Football was brilliant for me – I'll never forget how special that time was and I'll always appreciate the platform that it gave me to do other stuff. But that's all it is now: a platform for me. I'm a person who's moved on, and I'd like to be judged on that.

Writing this book should give an indication of not only how incredibly proud I am that I had my playing career, and that the values that the game taught me have helped me in my new life, but also that I'm not just a former footballer anymore. Hopefully, there are people out there that don't see me and immediately think of Wales or Everton, but remember how I've been able to help them or to connect them with someone who can.

I know that I can get on with kids. I know that I can build relationships with other people. I know that I can connect with others. I know that I can be someone that people are happy to open up to. I know that I can be a leader. I know that I can persuade people to get shit done. And I know that football helped me to be able to do all those things. And for this I will be forever grateful.

Perhaps the fact that I played before there were such vast sums of money in the game made that process of becoming something new much easier, because there was no choice for me but to keep working. Football served me really well, in that it gave me the tools and the ability to live comfortably for a while. But it didn't mean that I could become lazy, and it didn't automatically make me good at the job I do now – because that required hard work. I'm working harder now than I ever did at Everton, and that's a good thing.

I'd love to get involved in more of Everton's mental health initiatives. Although it might mean I'd be working seven days a week, it's something that I really want to do. The football side of things doesn't really bother me too much anymore, but the mental health and community side of it really excites me. When you learn that you can make a difference, or push people to make a difference, it becomes easy. It's so rewarding to see these positive changes. During the frustrating moments, these are what keep you enthused and make you want to do it. By the time this book is published, I will be almost 62. I do think about death and mortality a lot, and I think that's natural as you get older. Because of the books I read, often about people who have now passed away, it makes you consider your place in the world. What happens when someone gets a phone call one day to say that you have died? What happens to your stuff? What happens to those around you who you love? The reality is that nothing will happen. You're dead and that's that, and the people around you have to move on. Everyone will be around them for a week or two, and after six months everyone forgets to give a fuck because they have their own lives.

I'm really glad that my wife Emma has lots of friends around us, because that creates a support network. If I were to die tomorrow, I know that she would be able to get on – and remember me fondly. I think about having a daughter and a grandson, but what I've worked out is that nothing would happen. For them, life has to carry on. It's easier to die than to have someone around you die. You have nothing, you're gone. And as long as you have provided and prepared for those around you, your job is done.

I think about where I'd like to be buried. Would I like to be close to where my mum and dad are buried? Or do I want to be down here where I'm near Emma and she can visit the grave? But then why would you want to visit a grave? The person isn't there anyway, not really. It's just a piece of stone to mark the fact that you existed. You live on in their memories, and the life that they're able to go on and lead.

But while I'm still here, the challenge never ends and the work never stops. I want to go and work more and more in mental health. That has become the thing in this journey that has resonated with me and where I feel I can do the most good. Whether or not my time will run out before I can get as much done as I want, I don't know. But I'll do all I can, while I can.

These are the people in our society that most need help, those who suffer and struggle and for whom the funding doesn't exist to make their lives easier. I don't pretend to have all the answers, and I hope that this admission has become obvious throughout this book. But by accepting what I didn't and still don't know, I have been able to put myself in a position where I can help others. And if nothing else, I can connect them up so that we can create a huge network of contacts to help people across the world.

The one thing to come out of this desperate period in our lives, with lockdown and fear and the enforced reduction of our social interaction, is that it has reminded people about what really matters. We saw stories in our communities of people helping each other in times of need, and it would be brilliant if people can remember how important community spirit is when it finally passes.

I'm hoping that when people get back to normality they take lessons from the lockdown. People often say to me that they don't know what to do day by day, and that's because they aren't used to having large amounts of leisure time. So why should everyone kill themselves to work, work, work?

Working isn't the answer; life is the answer. Of course you need money, but let's try to make things more equal, so more people can be happy.

This should make people realise what life is truly about. It's about living your life the best you can and allowing others to do the same. People will realise what makes them happy and what doesn't make them happy, and realise that life is precious. You get 80 years if you're lucky, and there's no second chance, so this is a wake-up call to be happy and make those around you happy.

People show their true colours during times of crisis. There was greed, but there was also lots of great stuff going on too. After the initial panic, people began to look out for their neighbours and their friends and their extended families. We had a scheme on our road where if someone was going to the shops, they checked with everyone else if they needed anything. Now why can't that happen forever? It's a nice thing to do, it saves unnecessary car journeys and it cements a sense of community between people.

We've had that heart of the community ripped out over the last thirty years, and it has been deeply missed. We've been told to mistrust people, told that only money matters, been told to look after ourselves and nobody else, been told to step on people's heads to get what we want. But the pandemic has taught us a valuable lesson: we're far stronger when we come together than we ever could be apart.

I also hope it makes the population buy into the 'power of the people' principle. It's not the government that will get us through this mess, it's the people. It's the people working on frontline services, not the people in charge. So what I don't want to see after it's all done is politicians walking around like they're Winston fucking Churchill with cigars in their mouths slapping their mates on the back. Because if it wasn't for the goodness of the people, this crisis would have been a million times worse.

I think 2020 has made people appreciate the simple joy of being able to go outside their front door. Freedom of movement is hugely important. Just having the ability to go to work, to talk to people when you're there, and to come home again and have things to do and people to see – it puts the value of all that into sharp focus.

Before this crisis, the notion of community had largely been lost. People kept their heads down. Then suddenly, when you saw people if you were out exercising, everyone said good morning and hello, because they realised the importance of seeing other people. As long as we never lose sight of that again, we have a chance to be better.

It's also been really enjoyable to make a difference outside football, because I often think now about what really matters more. As a player you get to give enjoyment to supporters of club and country, and that's an absolute honour, but what *really* matters? I think what I do in my new life does, rather than what I did before. And that's what gives me the buzz. I've been able to have two lives, and have been recognised for something apart from football. I don't mean recognition from the papers or the media, because honestly that has never for one second been what it has been about for me. I mean recognition from the people I meet and the people I work with.

Something made me really happy the other day. I went to a community centre and someone said to me, 'I've heard really good things about you, and the things you're doing within the communities where you work.' That'll do for me. It's nothing about what I was, but who I am now. That's me going back to ground zero and becoming something new. If they've heard that I can make a difference, that's all I want.

ACKNOWLEDGEMENTS

In writing this book, it is only right that I thank a number of people, without whom it would not have been possible.

First, to Emma, my wife, who has listened to my inane drivel for years and continues to support me through everything. Thank you.

I have to thank Daniel Storey, who has worked with me on this book tirelessly, even when the circumstances of our normal life were turned upside down. Without him this wouldn't have been a book at all, and I thank him for listening to me talk for hours and turning those words into something I'm hugely proud of.

Thank you to all those people who provided quotes at the start of each chapter: Saiqa Naz, Asha Iqbal, Elizabeth Gregory, Sean Molino, Hope Virgo, Show Racism the Red Card, TransActual UK, Alan Wright, Kay Brophy and Philippa Davies. These people do incredible work in campaigning and assisting others, and it is an honour to have them included in the book.

Thank you to Anne-Marie Silbiger for her poems. Each of them was written solely for the purpose of this book, with Anne-Marie giving up her time to help create the moments of reflection that end each chapter.

Thanks to the publishers, HarperCollins, for taking on the project and helping turn it into something that I am extremely proud of.

And, finally, thank you to every person who reads this book. I hope that it can help you, and help you to help others.